51

Rethinking Information Literacy

A practical framework for supporting learning

Rethinking Information Literacy

A practical framework for supporting learning

Edited by

Jane Secker

and

Emma Coonan

 **facet publishing**

© This compilation: Jane Secker and Emma Coonan 2013
   The chapters: the contributors 2013

Published by Facet Publishing,
7 Ridgmount Street, London WC1E 7AE
www.facetpublishing.co.uk

Facet Publishing is wholly owned by CILIP: the Chartered Institute of
Library and Information Professionals.

British Library Cataloguing in Publication Data
A catalogue record for this book is available from the British Library.

ISBN 978-1-85604-822-4

First published 2013

Text printed on FSC accredited material.

Mixed Sources
Product group from well-managed
forests and other controlled sources
www.fsc.org Cert no. SA-COC-1565
© 1996 Forest Stewardship Council
FSC

Typeset from editors' files by Facet Publishing Production in 11.5/14pt
Garamond and Myriad Pro.
Printed and made in Great Britain by MPG Books Group, UK.

Contents

Acknowledgements

The editors are grateful to the Arcadia Project at the University of Cambridge for funding the research that led to the publication of this book. Thanks in particular to John Naughton for his support and input as our academic advisor, and for the suggestion that information literacy needed a new curriculum. We are also grateful to our employers for their support – Jane's at LSE and Emma's at Cambridge University Library – and to Wolfson College, Cambridge, which provided such a welcoming and intellectually stimulating environment in which to undertake our research.

We would both like to thank the contributors to this book, who illustrate ANCIL's principles in their own practice and who worked hard to meet our strict deadlines. Finally, particular thanks to Tim and Andrew for their patience during the writing of this book.

The screenshots on pages 32 and 37 are reproduced with permission from Newcastle University. The screenshots on pages 82-90 are reproduced with permission from the University of Sheffield.

Jane Secker and Emma Coonan

Contributor profiles

Moira Bent MA BSc NTF
Moira Bent is Faculty Liaison Librarian at Newcastle University, and a National Teaching Fellow. A liaison librarian for many years, the National Teaching Fellowship enabled her to develop her research interests in information literacy, international student support and services for research. As well as publishing several journal articles, she is co-author of *The Informed Researcher* (Vitae, 2012), the SCONUL 'Seven Pillars of Information Literacy' model (SCONUL, 2011), *Providing Effective Library Services for Research* (Facet Publishing, 2007) and the SCONUL 'Guidelines on Library Services for International Students' (2008). She is a member of the SCONUL Working Group on Information Literacy and the RIN Information Handling Skills Advocacy Group. Her blog is at www.moirabent.blogspot.com.

Jamie Cleland BA MSc PhD Learning Excellence Fellow
Dr Jamie Cleland joined Staffordshire University in September 2005 and is Senior Lecturer in Sport Sociology. He achieved his PhD from the University of Liverpool in 2008. Jamie's main research and publications have focused on the sociological significance of sport on supporters, players, the local community, organizations, consumption and the media. He also writes on contemporary cultural issues such as volunteering, race and gender and how audiences engage and interact with the developing media. He has published in *Sport and Social Issues, Ethnic and Racial Studies, Soccer and Society*, the *International Journal of Sport Communication* and *Media, Culture and Society*.

Emma Coonan MSt PhD MSc

Dr Emma Coonan directs and teaches on Cambridge University's Research Skills Programme (www.lib.cam.ac.uk/courses), which supports the information skills and academic development of students and researchers across the university. She holds a PhD in literary theory as well as an MSc in Information and Library Management. Her chief research interests are information literacy and learning development, and in 2011 she was seconded to a fellowship at Wolfson College, Cambridge, to develop 'A New Curriculum for Information Literacy' in collaboration with Jane Secker. In 2012 she was nominated for Information Literacy Practitioner of the Year.

Emma blogs as The Mongoose Librarian (http://librariangoddess. wordpress.com) and tweets as @LibGoddess.

Isla Kuhn MA MSc

Never having imagined working in the health and medical library world, Isla Kuhn surprised herself when she got a job in the Cairns Library, University of Oxford's medical library based at the John Radcliffe Hospital. She's never looked back. A move to the University of Leicester allowed her to set up and run a library outreach service for primary care and mental healthcare NHS staff working across Leicestershire and Rutland.

Taking up her post at University of Cambridge Medical Library in 2005 allowed Isla to return to the mixed worlds of higher education and direct patient care. There are plenty of opportunities to contribute to education, learning, research and clinical care across both the university and Addenbrooke's Hospital, and to collaborate with colleagues from higher education (HE) and the NHS. Providing support to student doctors, postgraduate researchers and clinical staff ensures that every day is different.

Isla's professional interests include Web 2.0 applications in library, educational and clinical settings and developing the educational role of librarians. She is a founder member of the first librarian TeachMeet, which encourages sharing of expertise in an informal setting.

Clare McCluskey BA (Hons) MSc PGCert MCLIP FHEA

Clare McCluskey has worked in academic libraries since 2001 and in an academic librarian role since 2008, focusing on enquiry services prior to this. She is currently academic support librarian for the Faculty of Education and Theology at York St John University, where she is also a University Teaching

Fellow. She has carried out action research into the concept of librarians as educators and partners in HE, presenting at both educational research conferences and those for information professionals. She is particularly interested in the concept of communities of practice in relation to information literacy, both within HE libraries and across departments in HE institutions.

Lyn Parker BA MEd PGDip MCLIP

Lyn Parker is Head of Learning and Teaching Enhancement and Copyright Compliance Officer at the University of Sheffield Library. Her present role involves information literacy, copyright awareness and support for e-learning and blended learning. She has previously worked as an academic development librarian, a liaison librarian and a site librarian. She is currently Secretary of CILIP: the Chartered Institute of Library and Information Professionals CSG Information Literacy Group and a member of the Universities UK/GuildHE Copyright Working Group. She is particularly interested in the use of social media and emerging technologies and how these impact on information literacy, research skills and the design of learning spaces.

Sarah Pavey MSc FCLIP

Sarah Pavey is Senior Librarian at Box Hill School, and holds a degree in Biochemistry and a Masters in Information Science. She has worked as a school librarian for over 15 years both in the independent and maintained sectors. She has written *Going Digital* (a guide to IT for primary school libraries) published in 2011 by the School Library Association, is co-author of *The Innovative School Librarian: thinking outside the box* (published by Facet in 2009) and has spoken at numerous library conferences. She is also an independent library consultant and conducts regular training events for CILIP, the School Library Association, the Special Schools and Academies Trust and the International Baccalaureate.

Andy Priestner BA MA MCLIP

Andy Priestner is Information and Library Services Manager at Cambridge University's Judge Business School, where he has made radical changes to resource provision and service levels. He was Chair of the UK's Business Librarians Association from 2006 to 2010 (which was rebranded and relaunched during his tenure). In 2007 he was awarded a teaching excellence award by the University of Oxford. In 2010 he led the 23 Things social media programme for Cambridge University library staff. He has recently co-edited the book *Personalising Library Services in Higher Education* for Ashgate Publishing and contributed a case study to Ned Potter's *The Library Marketing Toolkit* (Facet Publishing, 2012).

Jane Secker BA (Joint Hons) PhD PGCert(HE) FHEA
Dr Jane Secker is the Copyright and Digital Literacy Advisor at the London School of Economics and Political Science. She works in the Centre for Learning Technology, which is a small team supporting staff and researchers in their use of technology to enhance teaching and learning. She co-ordinates a digital literacy programme and provides copyright advice and training.

Jane is Editor of the *Journal of Information Literacy* and was Conference Officer for the CILIP CSG Information Literacy group from 2004 to 2012, organizing the Librarians' Information Literacy Annual Conference (LILAC), which has grown to be an international conference attracting over 300 delegates from around the world. She has published widely on information literacy, e-learning and copyright issues and has undertaken research on libraries and social media.

Elizabeth Tilley PGCE MA MSc FHEA
Elizabeth Tilley has worked in small, specialist academic libraries since 1997; her previous career as a trained teacher has helped to inform much of her work in libraries. Currently working in the English Faculty Library at the University of Cambridge, she has made many changes to the library service – policies, look and feel, teaching, and use of space – in order to tailor the service appropriately to student needs and specific student groups. This is especially evident in the teaching programmes that are now in place.

Elizabeth is committed to the profession and has been active at both national and international levels via CILIP. She is a Fellow of the Higher Education Academy.

Geoff Walton BA (Joint Hons) MA PgCHPE PhD FHEA MCLIP Learning Excellence Fellow
Dr Geoff Walton is a Senior Researcher and Academic Skills Tutor: Librarian at Staffordshire University. Geoff is interested in the cognitive and metacognitive processes involved in becoming information literate and how

information behaviour theory and research can help understand these. He contributes to the working group which develops the Assignment Survival Kit or ASK (www.staffs.ac.uk/ask). Geoff is extending his research interests into bibliometrics, social media and digital literacy, and is also interested in identifying synergies between information literacy, e-learning and inquiry-based learning. He was SLA Europe Information Professional 2010. He is joint managing editor of the online journal *Innovative Practice in Higher Education* (www.staffs.ac.uk/ipihe) and member of the Research Information Network (RIN) Information Handling Group (now rebranded as the Research, information and Digital Literacies Coalition – RiDLS).

Helen Webster BA (Hons) MA DPhil PGCE

Dr Helen Webster researched and lectured in Modern Languages, with a DPhil and teaching profile in Medieval German Literature, until 2005. Her increasing interest in teaching and learning, built on her PGCE in Higher Education, led her to become a learning developer in a student services role. She was Coordinator for the Learning Enhancement Team at the University of East Anglia, before becoming a Research Associate at the University of Cambridge, working on projects to support and develop student learning. She has experience of working across all disciplines and with students at every level of HE, from pre-sessional to PhD and PostDocs, and very much enjoys interprofessional collaboration with colleagues from other areas of HE.

Katy Wrathall BA (Hons)

Katy Wrathall worked in IT for 15 years before undertaking the BA in Library and Information Management at Manchester Metropolitan University (MMU), where she attained First Class Honours and two Dun & Bradstreet Awards. She then worked for Lancashire Schools Library Service (Project Loans), followed by a temporary post as lecturer at MMU on Information Users.

Katy worked in Herefordshire College of Technology's Learning Resources Centres for several years, latterly as Learning Resources Centres Manager. She then became Project Manager for the SMILE blended learning project at University of Worcester with Imperial College London and Loughborough University, at the same time undertaking two contracts as Academic Liaison Team Leader during periods of transition. Since completing the project she has undertaken consultancy at Glasgow

Caledonian University on implementing SMILE. Katy is also an Arcadia Fellow of Wolfson College, Cambridge, where she investigated 'Implementing a New Curriculum for Information Literacy in non-Cambridge Higher Education Institutions'. She is currently Academic Services Team Leader at York St John University.

Introduction

We live in the age of information, where the physical, economic and social barriers that previously stemmed the flow of knowledge have been largely broken down by the internet and related technologies. This is the digital age, where computers and technologies are supremely powerful and the potential that they offer to human endeavour and particularly to education is great. However, in this world of digital information it is more critical than ever before to ensure that citizens of the world are information literate. People need the skills and values to enable them not just to access information but to use it to make informed judgements and choices, to make their voices heard and make a difference. Librarians have recognized this for many years and call these skills and values 'information literacy'.

Information-literate people are discerning in their choice of information sources and their use of knowledge. They are judicious citizens who can use information to transform their circumstances, create new knowledge and reach their full potential. There is a growing recognition that simply providing access to information through digital technology is not enough. There is a need to develop individuals with the ability to ask questions of the information they find and to evaluate sources critically. These abilities are recognized by UNESCO as human rights, fundamental to democracy (UNESCO, 2005) and they should be a goal for educators everywhere.

Information literacy is particularly crucial for young people as they progress through school, further and higher education and into the place of work, but we also must ensure that everyone, whether retired or working, young or old, rich or poor, is equipped with these vital abilities. Educators are preparing children and young people for a world in which change is inevitable. Computing power has developed at such a speed that tasks that previously required large computers filling a room can now be undertaken using a device that fits in our pockets. It is a seemingly impossible task for teachers to prepare the child born in 2012 for careers and professions that they cannot imagine. Yet if the pace of technological development over the past 25 years continues, our need for an increasingly skilled and digitally literate population will only become more critical. However, for the most part, the education sector has failed to recognize the crucial role that information literacy plays in human development.

The world has moved from an industrial society to an information society. In the UK and much of the developed world we operate in a knowledge economy where what and who you know, how quickly you can respond to change, and the ability to make decisions quickly and efficiently and solve problems, are all critically important. Yet we are living in a world where access to information through technology is unprecedented. Answers to questions are seemingly at the end of our fingertips – and very soon voice recognition technologies might make even our fingertips redundant. Yet in a world awash with information and knowledge, young people appear increasingly unable to carry out independent research, reluctant to argue and to challenge big ideas and to take risks to discover new knowledge. Instead they readily copy and paste ideas rather than read and critique them. In the UK we might blame this on the formal education system which has been criticized for focusing largely on assessing the recall of facts. Formal education systems mean that testing and exams become the focus of the teacher and the learner in schools, at the expense of developing our learner's inquiring minds.

However, this is not a state that teachers, parents, employers and governments are happy with. In fact, there is considerable concern and a growing awareness about this situation and the problems it might be causing. A recent report by Demos on young people's critical use of the internet suggested that helping them navigate hugely variable internet sources should be achieved not by tighter controls, but by ensuring that students can make informed judgements about the information they find (Bartlett and Miller, 2011, 4). In the quest to develop students who think critically about information and have a thirst for knowledge, a small but increasingly vocal band of librarians has been battling for many years. Their information literacy initiatives are much to be admired and in some cases within their own institutions they may be recognized formally for their contribution. However, sadly, this is not the case everywhere, and this is not helped by a perception in the mainstream media that equates librarians with books and out of step with the modern world. In reading this book you might be forgiven, then, for asking yourself if information literacy might therefore be the saviour of the library. If librarians are not needed to manage books, perhaps they can evolve into a new role as information literacy experts?

This book was written as the library profession faces a future in which there will be unprecedented access to information. However, the challenges of the new information environment should concern everyone in the education sector: in schools, further and higher education, the skills sector and workplace learning. Therefore, if you are a librarian reading this book we urge you to pass it on to a teacher or a lecturer, or better still a principal or dean or even an education policy maker. For this book needs to be read by policy makers and by those who hold the power to change education for the better. Governments need to recognize (as UNESCO does) that information and digitally literate people are vital for a successful and democratic society and they are vital for the economy.

This book examines more granular issues but also suggests a more central role for librarians as teachers and the library as a learning space in the digital age. For many years librarians themselves have seen their role as being around collection building and knowledge organization, often based upon books. However, in the digital age we need to be curators of information and knowledge in all its forms. Books are simply a format in which human knowledge and endeavour can be recorded. But libraries are not merely repositories of information, collected for posterity. Libraries have a fundamental role in providing access to information and knowledge, to enable it to be used and communicated to others. In essence, libraries – whether they are public or academic libraries, school libraries or in the workplace – facilitate learning. Learning enables research and research brings about transformation and progress. This book therefore positions libraries, librarians and information literacy at the heart of the development of society. In the digital age, the librarian must take a more central role in providing access to knowledge and information, and recognize their role as a facilitator of learning.

And what of the role of the teacher in the age of disintermediated access

XVIII   RETHINKING INFORMATION LITERACY

to an unprecedented volume of information? Knowledge contained in books used to be a scarce commodity only available to a privileged few in universities who had access to large libraries. However, technological developments, alongside movements such as open education (e.g. www.oercommons.org/) and open access publishing,[1] are changing this. We are also seeing the rise of the 'digital scholar' (Weller, 2011) as social media allow us all to interchange between being creators, curators and consumers of information. In this new information landscape some writers (e.g. Godin, 2011) recognize the role of the librarian as important, trusted guides and libraries as trusted sources of information. The more traditional view of libraries as 'walled gardens' often seems unhelpful, elitist and out of step with the open education and open access agenda. While librarians may no longer be gatekeepers of knowledge, they can be valuable trusted guides and through information literacy initiatives they can help learners become autonomous and able to make their own informed judgements. None of us knows what the future holds for libraries: it is only through research such as this might we develop an understanding and plan appropriately.

The changes we are urging in this book are quite subtle and do not require radically changing everything that we do, but in rethinking information literacy we must recognize that librarians are not islands in the education sphere. Neither are they the owners of 'information literacy'. That may be seen by some as revolutionary, but if we are truly committed to information literacy we will recognize that it is too important to remain the preserve of the library. We must seek out partnerships to work interprofessionally in our schools, colleges and universities. We must ensure that the new curriculum for information literacy has support at the highest level in our organizations. And we must lobby policy makers to ensure that governments recognize the central importance of information literacy in learning. Only then can we work towards the shared ambition of developing autonomous, lifelong learners who are able to use information effectively in their academic studies and in their personal and professional lives.

Background to ANCIL development

This book was inspired by research undertaken at the University of Cambridge as part of the Arcadia Programme. Arcadia funded 20 fellowships that allowed librarians and researchers to take time out from their regular activities to explore the role of academic libraries in the digital age.[2] John Naughton, who at the time was Professor of the Public Understanding of Technology at the Open University, was the project's academic adviser. From May to July in 2011 two librarians were chosen to work on a joint fellowship and through this research partnership A New Curriculum for Information Literacy, or ANCIL, was born (Coonan and Secker, 2011).

The original research brief was to develop a practical curriculum for information literacy that would meet the needs of undergraduate students entering higher education over the next five years. Specifically the project aimed:

- to understand the information needs of future undergraduate students on entering higher education
- to develop a revolutionary curriculum for information literacy that can be used with undergraduate students entering UK higher education
- to provide practical guidance about how best to equip students with the knowledge, skills and behaviour around information use to support their learning in the digital age
- to develop a flexible curriculum that can be used and adapted in the higher education community and used in face-to-face, blended and online learning provision.

The timescale for the project was ten weeks, so this partly dictated how the research was undertaken. The methods chosen included an extensive review of the literature, to provide a Theoretical Background to the research (Coonan, 2011). This was accompanied by a modified Delphi study (Secker, 2011) that involved consulting experts in the information and education field on the content and nature of an information literacy curriculum for the future. Interviews and questionnaires were used to gather the opinions of the group and these were analysed and coded. Perhaps surprisingly, the experts suggested that the way the curriculum was delivered was at least as important as the topics that it included. Using findings from the literature and from the interviews and questionnaires a draft curriculum was drawn up and presented to the expert group during a one-day workshop. Feedback was gathered throughout the day and the curriculum was subsequently refined and finalized, to be released in July 2011 with a number of supporting documents. Three reports in addition to the curriculum itself are available from the project website[3] and they have all been licensed for re-use under Creative Commons licences.

The outputs of the initial ANCIL project attracted considerable attention in the information profession and the Arcadia Programme was keen to explore how the curriculum might work in practice. Consequently, Arcadia agreed to fund a follow-up project from October to December 2011, to explore strategies for implementing the new curriculum.[4] Helen Webster carried out research at the University of Cambridge to explore how the curriculum could inform the development of teaching resources. Meanwhile Katy Wrathall worked with the University of Worcester and at York St John University to explore how ANCIL could be used to audit information literacy provision at institutional level. The main outputs of their project are available on a wiki,[5] including a range of resources to audit provision at an institutional level and to support practice on the ground. We were also delighted that both the authors agreed to contribute to this book.

In the past year ANCIL has been presented at a number of international conferences, and is being used by several UK universities as a method of auditing their information literacy provision across the entire institution. Perhaps more importantly, however, ANCIL is proving to be a valuable framework for librarians to redefine information literacy and set their teaching and support provision within a wider, more learner-focused perspective. The research suggests it is helpful to frame information literacy as a key element within learning development, and the curriculum helps to support the transformation that takes place in students from the time they enter university to when they graduate.

Definition, terminology, the information literacy landscape

The term 'information literacy' was first used almost 40 years ago and was coined by Paul Zurkowski, a US librarian (Zurkowski, 1974). Since this time there have been numerous definitions of information literacy as well as frameworks and models developed around the world by library professional bodies such as the Australian and New Zealand Institute for Information Literacy (ANZIL), the Association of College and Research Libraries (ACRL) and SCONUL (the Society of College, National and University Libraries).[6] In some countries we have also seen attempts, largely driven by the library sector, to develop national frameworks for information literacy at a government level such as the Welsh Information Literacy Framework.[7]

However, perhaps the broadest and most ambitious definition of information literacy that influenced ANCIL comes from UNESCO. Working in partnership with the National Forum on Information Literacy,[8] UNESCO issued the Prague Declaration on information literacy in 2003 and followed this in 2005 by the Alexandria Proclamation. UNESCO believe that:

> Information literacy empowers people in all walks of life to seek, evaluate, use and create information effectively to achieve their personal, social, occupational and educational goals. It is a basic human right in a digital world and promotes social inclusion in all nations.
>
> UNESCO (2005)

In the space of this introductory chapter it is not possible to provide a comprehensive overview of the literature on information literacy, nor is it necessary, as this can be found in the Theoretical Background report to ANCIL (Coonan, 2011). However, it is worth briefly describing some of the key issues. In particular, our research found that almost all definitions recognize information literacy as an important element of learner autonomy, underpinning both formal and lifelong learning. Yet a major chasm exists between the aspirational assertions outlined in these definitions and the applied teaching of information literacy in UK educational institutions. Arguably this is mainly due to a failure to establish a common framework of terminology (Coonan, 2011, 5). It is also clear that the term 'information literacy', which has been at time contentious within the library profession, is seemingly invisible to those outside it. This invisibility is particularly evident amongst faculty, teachers and experienced researchers. A number of explanations have been given, including the separation of the functional and intellectual aspects of information, a confusion between information literacy and IT literacy, and assumptions about the capabilities of the Google Generation (Coonan, 2011).

What is clear is that information literacy comes in many guises and the term has obvious overlaps with concepts such as academic literacies, digital literacy, media literacy, transliteracy and new literacy. It has also been called 'digital fluency', 'information capabilities' or 'information competencies', but as Badke notes, 'the literature of information literacy remains in the library silo' (2010, 129).

Finally, there is a significant correspondence or consonance between information literacy and high-level intellectual operations such as critical thinking, problem solving, question framing and independent learning. In

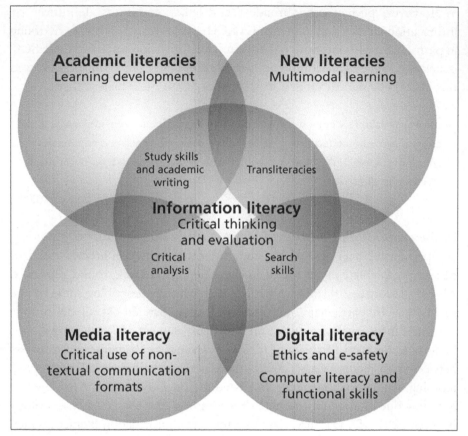

Figure 0.1   *The information literacy landscape*

Figure 0.1 we illustrate of this information literacy landscape, reflecting the overlapping terminology.

At the end of the ANCIL research project it seemed appropriate to offer a new definition of information literacy, echoing the UNESCO definition, but one that summarized our thinking:

> Information literacy is a continuum of skills, behaviours, approaches and values that it is so deeply entwined with the use of information as to be a fundamental part of learning, scholarship and research. It is the defining characteristics of the discerning scholar, the informed and judicious citizen and the autonomous learner.[9]

What makes ANCIL different?

One of the first questions Katy Wrathall and Helen Webster asked when tasked with implementing the curriculum was 'If this is the new curriculum, can we see the old one?' There is no old curriculum. The library profession has developed standards and models, but the new curriculum is different because it offers the teacher a series of practical steps through which to scaffold the individual's development of a reflective learning framework. In designing our curriculum we were heavily influenced by the work of Biggs (1996), who advocates a process of 'constructive alignment' to ensure that curriculum content is closely aligned with not only the intended learning outcomes, but also the assessment mechanisms and learning activities employed to achieve these outcomes. Our curriculum has intended learning outcomes, it has activities and it has assessment, and we have aligned these to develop the skills, behaviours and knowledge that we want in our students.

The curriculum is divided into ten strands, which cover the whole landscape of information literacy development required to succeed as an undergraduate in higher education. The strands are most clearly represented visually (see Figure 0.2) but comprise:

1 Transition from school to higher education.
2 Becoming an independent learner.
3 Developing academic literacies.
4 Mapping and evaluating the information landscape.
5 Resource discovery in your discipline.
6 Managing information.
7 The ethical dimension of information.
8 Presenting and communicating knowledge.
9 Synthesizing information and creating new knowledge.
10 The social dimension of information.

Strands One and Ten, which book-end the curriculum, link reflective learning with specific transition points in the undergraduate career. Strand One focuses on the transition from school to higher education – a perfect time to engage students in their own learning process by giving them a vocabulary and analytic structure through which to address the significant changes in expectations, teaching styles and attitudes towards learning that occur at this point. Strand Ten deals with transferring information literacy skills,

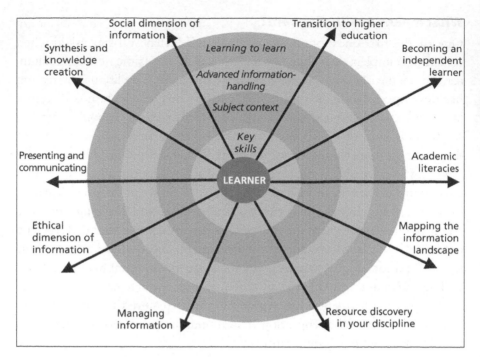

Figure 0.2 *The ANCIL ten strands*

behaviours and attitudes to everyday life, in line with the principles of lifelong learning.

Strand Two, in contrast, is not linked to a specific transition point. Rather, it is informed by the idea that change occurs throughout the learning process as a natural, unavoidable and sometimes challenging aspect of learning. The content of Strand Two is iterative and reflective, and aims to give students ongoing, scaffolded support as they develop the conceptual and intellectual infrastructure for assimilating new information over the course of their undergraduate career. The concept of 'scaffolding' is described in detail by Walton and Cleland in Strand Two of this book. The focus in this strand (as in Strands One and Ten) is on learning to learn.

Strand Three aims to explore and develop the academic literacies of reading and writing at both the functional, procedural level – skimming and scanning strategies, recognizing and using appropriate academic idiom – and in higher-order activities, such as textual interrogation and critiquing, argument construction and understanding of a discipline's epistemological structure and values. It encourages a reflective understanding of academic literacies as the performance of a socially constructed practice and one to which they can bring their prior experience, skills and values.

Strands Four and Five focus on dealing with subject-specific information and many librarians may feel particularly comfortable teaching these strands. Strand Five is intended to familiarize students with specialist resources of various types and content in their discipline, while Strand Four focuses on developing awareness and understanding of the range of source types available and how to evaluate them for reliability, authority and their appropriateness for the student's specific purpose. The underlying aim of these strands is to enable students to become familiar with the information landscape of their discipline.

Strand Six focuses on practical, functional skills to manage information, many of which will be recognizable in existing library instruction courses. These remain key skills without which students will struggle to find, select, manage and process academic information efficiently. In many cases a huge range of software and online tools is available to simplify these processes. We have not stipulated particular tools to teach, firstly since technology is moving at too fast a pace, and secondly in order to emphasize that understanding the process itself is as important as being aware of tools or programs designed to aid the process.

Strands Seven, Eight and Nine deal with the high-order cognitive and intellectual functions of information handling. These include critiquing and analysing material, synthesizing viewpoints, formulating research questions, and the ethical dimension of information use and production. These facets have traditionally been perceived as belonging to the academic province; however, as discussed in both the ANCIL Theoretical Background (Coonan, 2011) and the Expert Consultation Report (Secker, 2011), a holistic view of information literacy advocates that separating 'functional' skills and high-order abilities occludes the research process and disadvantages the student.

Within each strand of information literacy the learner develops through four broad levels or bands, operating at successively more sophisticated cognitive levels. It is strongly recommended that every class relating to information literacy should contain an element corresponding to each of the four bands:

• key skills
• subject-specific competences

- advanced information handling
- learning to learn.

To support this multi-faceted development, ANCIL identifies four learning bands to which information literacy class content should be aligned. Thus each session not only contains a practical skills element but also looks at the subject context in which the skill is deployed, together with its application within higher-level information-handling operations such as critical evaluation, synthesis and problem framing. Finally, each session should contain opportunities for the student to reflect on how the skills, abilities and insights gained can be employed elsewhere in their academic practice, or even beyond.

These strands are not intended to form ten discrete modules or classes. Their content should be incorporated into the academic curriculum as appropriate to the needs of the discipline. They can also be combined in a variety of ways, and specific learning outcomes and activities are presented to guide those tasked with implementation. A variety of other resources, including examples of good practice, an evidence toolkit and a mapping of the new curriculum to existing models of information literacy, were developed in Phase One to assist in implementation. We have included a selection of these resources in the appendices, including the full curriculum (Appendix 1), a worksheet to assist in lesson planning (Appendix 2) and resources to carry out an institutional audit (Appendices 3 and 4). Further resources are available online.

Rethinking information literacy: the case studies

Coonan and Secker's 2011 research positioned information literacy as a vital, holistic and institution-wide element in academic teaching and learning. Rather than taking a competency-based approach in which abilities and performance levels are mandated prescriptively, ANCIL is founded on a perception of information literacy as a continuum of skills, competences, behaviours and values around information, centred on an individual learner engaged in a specific task or moving towards a particular goal. The ANCIL research revealed some key issues associated with information literacy, one of the most important of which was the finding that the way in which information literacy is perceived, taught and implemented at institutional level is as important as the topics that are covered. Furthermore, information literacy needs to be embedded into the academic curriculum as far as possible; it also needs to be ongoing throughout a student's academic career and adapted according to the specific requirements of the discipline.

The chapters in this book, each written by a practitioner in the field, reflect the diversity of disciplines taught in higher education, from Business Studies (Strand Eight), to English (Strand Six), to Medicine (Strand Five) to Education (Strand Four). However, they each usefully illustrate some of the key attributes of our curriculum. In Strands Three, Seven and Ten, Moira Bent, Lyn Parker and Helen Webster all describe how information literacy is embedded in the curriculum at their respective institutions. In Strands Six and Eight, Elizabeth Tilley and Andy Priestner describe flexible approaches to the sessions they teach. Meanwhile, Emma Coonan (Strand Nine) and Isla Kuhn (Strand Five) describe how their teaching reflects a holistic approach to the research process. Collaboration between academics and learning support staff is a key theme in the new curriculum, and Clare McCluskey describes building effective partnerships in Strand Four.

The curriculum needs to include opportunities for students to work collaboratively and to reflect on their learning. It should be based on real needs, ascertained by auditing learners' prior experience of information contexts. In Strand One, Sarah Pavey describes the information literacy teaching that takes place in her school to prepare students for independent learning, which hints at some of the transition issues that students experience when entering higher education. Meanwhile, assessment forms an important part of this curriculum, although we recognize that information literacy can be difficult to assess summatively. In this respect, approaches such as the peer assessment activity outlined by Geoff Walton and Jamie Cleland in Strand Two are helpful.

The ANCIL research demonstrates that the new curriculum must be interprofessional, not restricted to the library, and therefore needs to be taught collaboratively by a range of staff members within an institution. This includes librarians, learning developers, IT and e-learning staff, together with academic staff. A programme of staff development such as that described by Moira Bent in Strand Three is therefore required to equip staff within an institution with the understanding and skills they need to deliver the curriculum. In order to be most effective, the curriculum needs buy-in from senior management. Therefore it must be clear how information literacy relates to the strategic aims of the institution, such as graduate capabilities, employability, enhancing the student experience and improving achievement. In Strand Ten by Helen Webster we see examples from a learning development perspective that suggest ways that the link between information literacy and lifelong learning can be made explicit to learners.

Since undertaking our research it has become clear that valuable work in information literacy beyond that illustrated in this book is being undertaken by library and information professionals that supports and illustrates the ANCIL approach. We do not suggest that institutions, teachers and librarians need to fundamentally change much of what they are currently doing. Rather, ANCIL is designed to help you rethink and reposition what you are doing in terms of information literacy provision, whether in taught sessions, online, or in informal, ad hoc support. We hope it may help you to consider reviewing or auditing who provides support in your own institution, what overlaps may exist, and what gaps there might be in provision from the student's point of view. We also hope it will assist you in rethinking information literacy as a fundamental part of the learning process, which needs to be embedded firmly within an academic discipline, but which requires specialist knowledge and understanding to teach.

Conclusion

This book presents a range of case studies illustrating each of the ten strands of ANCIL to show where good practice is occurring already across the UK. Ten practitioners from a range of institutions describe their work in the context of ANCIL, illustrating each strand's content with a description of a practical resource, tool or approach, an outline of how this supports the development of independent learning, and a brief overview of the pedagogic principles that guide them. We would like to collect further examples of good practice, so do consider submitting a case study to the websites that accompany this book. For those of you interested in following the progress of ANCIL, we have set up a blog and a mailing list, and for those of you who would like to share your resources or use any that we have developed which are licensed under Creative Commons, we have established a wiki.[10]

We wrote this book to inspire librarians to think about the big picture when they teach or support library users, whoever they might be. But we also wrote it to broaden understanding about what information literacy is, about why it is so important in education and about the role that librarians can play in developing and supporting learners. We hope by the time you have finished reading it we might have gone some way towards achieving our ambitions.

Notes

1 See www.soros.org/openaccess/, www.arl.org/sparc/.
2 http://arcadiaproject.lib.cam.ac.uk/historical.html.
3 http://newcurriculum.wordpress.com.
4 http://arcadiaproject.lib.cam.ac.uk/projects/strategies-for-implementation.html.
5 http://implementingancil.pbworks.com.
6 oil.otago.ac.nz/oil/index/ANZIIL-Standards.html;
   www.ala.org/acrl/standards/informationliteracycompetency;
   www.sconul.ac.uk/groups/information_literacy/seven_pillars.html.
7 http://welshinformationliteracy.org.
8 http://infolit.org.
9 From our blog post, http://new curriculum.wordpress.com/2012/01/13/blue-skies-a-new-definition-of-information-literacy/.
10 Blog and mailing list available at http://newcurriculum.wordpress.com; wiki at http://implementingancil.pbworks.com.

Bibliography

Badke, W. (2010) Why Information Literacy is Invisible, *Communications in Information Literacy*, **4** (2), 129–41.

Bartlett, J. and Miller, C. (2011) *Truth, Lies and the Internet: a report into young people's digital fluency*, Demos, www.demos.co.uk/publications/truth-lies-and-the-internet.

Biggs, J. (1996) Enhancing Teaching Through Constructive Alignment, *Higher Education*, **32** (3), 347–64.

Coonan, E. (2011) *Teaching Learning: perceptions of information literacy*, http://newcurriculum.wordpress.com/project-reports-and-outputs/.

Coonan, E. and Secker, J. (2011) *A New Curriculum for Information Literacy: curriculum and supporting documents*, http://newcurriculum.wordpress.com/project-reports-and-outputs/.

Godin, Seth (2011) The Future of the Library, *Seth's Blog*, http://sethgodin.typepad.com/seths_blog/2011/05/the-future-of-the-library.html.

Secker, J. (2011) *A New Curriculum for Information Literacy: expert consultation report*, http:// newcurriculum.wordpress.com/project-reports-and-outputs.

UNESCO (2005) *Beacons of the Information Society: the Alexandria Proclamation on information literacy and lifelong learning*,
http://archive.ifla.org/III/wsis/BeaconInfSoc.html.

Weller, M. (2011) *The Digital Scholar: how technology is transforming scholarly practice*, Bloomsbury.

Zurkowski, P. (1974) *The Information Environment: relationships and priorities*, National Commission on Libraries and Information Science, Washington, DC.

Strand One

Transition from school to higher education

Sarah Pavey

Strand One, unusually, links an aspect of information literacy learning to a specific point in the undergraduate career. The content of this strand focuses on the transition from school to higher education – a perfect time to engage students in their own learning process by giving them a vocabulary and analytic structure through which to address the significant changes in expectations, teaching styles and attitudes to learning that occur at this point. This deeply reflective opportunity is mirrored by the content of Strand Ten, which supports the transition to the workplace and everyday life. Book-ending the curriculum, these strands deal with the transference of information literacy skills, behaviours and attitudes to new cultures, and with ongoing exploration and development of the learner's identity in relation to information contexts.

Sarah took part in the expert consultation carried out as part of the ANCIL research and was chosen because she is a qualified librarian working in the independent school sector. In many ways her experience is atypical, as the demands of the International Baccalaureate, which are very different from those of A-levels, explicitly help students make the transition into higher education. Sarah's approach to information literacy, and the learning culture at Box Hill School, form a sound basis for helping students make the transition to the higher education environment. In particular, her teaching makes explicit the transitional issues that need to be addressed when students move through school and into higher education.

Institutional context

Box Hill School is an independent co-educational, part-boarding school for students aged 11–19 years, and also has an International Study Centre.

Twenty-five countries are represented among its 425 students, and many staff have experience of teaching abroad.

The school follows the philosophy of Kurt Hahn, experimental educationalist and founder of Gordonstoun. It helped to initiate Round Square (www.roundsquare.org), a worldwide association of more than 80 schools. Students are committed to participating in the six pillars, or IDEALS: International understanding; Democracy; Environment; Adventure; Leadership; and Service.

In 2008 the decision was taken to abandon the traditional English syllabus in favour of the International Baccalaureate Diploma (IB). The International Baccalaureate Organisation (IBO) requires any school it endorses for the Diploma to have a library, and recommends that this library be managed by a qualified teacher-librarian (IBO, 2004). In May 2008 I was appointed to create a new library and to develop independent learning throughout the school.

Students join the school at one of three stages. The youngest intake is 11 years old, Year 7 (Key Stage 3). Preparatory schools in the UK can retain students until the end of Year 8 (age 13) when they sit the Common Entrance Examination and join our school in Year 9 (Key Stage 3 to Key Stage 4 transition). The oldest students join the sixth form, aged 16. They sometimes undertake a pre-IB year to improve their language skills. Any information literacy and teaching of skills for independent learning must take these divisions into account. This chapter will describe each of the approaches adopted and the outcomes.

Transitions at school level

In the primary sector there are not many formal libraries: a qualified information specialist is a luxury only a small number can afford. Hence, few students gain any knowledge of research skills as we know them. A bad habit transferring with these students is a sense that reward is for presentation rather than content. There is a copy and paste culture present in most work and an abundance of irrelevant images and zany fonts to make their work 'look nice'. As the Demos report (Bartlett and Miller, 2011) confirms, there is little evidence of evaluation, synthesis and understanding. At Box Hill School we are aware that parents question the degree of 'learning' that takes place in this type of 'research' homework.

At our school it is important to try and retain as many of our students as possible in the sixth form. Students believe the Diploma is 'hard work' in comparison with the more traditional A-levels. Much of this stems from the emphasis the Diploma places on independent work and critical thinking. This may be why IB Diploma students fare well in higher education (Higher Education Statistics Agency, 2011). We feel it is imperative to teach these skills throughout the school to ensure our students stay until they leave to higher education.

Herring's (2009) research looks at how younger secondary students can be taught to use good information skills as evidenced by outcome. In our own collaborative action research with Year 8 (Pavey and Monk, 2012) we found a basic platform in information skills led to an intrinsic curiosity about the topic. Murdock and Anderman (2006) demonstrate that intrinsic motivation can lessen plagiarism. Initial findings of our study show that it is essential for both teacher and librarian to work closely together to gain the best results. We used formative assessment to mark work alongside the student rather than simply giving a grade. We gave verbal and written feedback. This, too, engendered a desire to improve that was self-motivated. The standard of work produced was very high and written in a formal academic style, with illustrations correctly titled and supporting the text.

Another distinct group are students taking GCSE examinations at Key Stage 4 (age 14–15). The very nature of this examination does not reward information literacy and it is hard to build upon what has been covered in earlier years. The government has argued that A-level papers should be set by universities rather than examination boards to ensure that students meet the criteria expected at undergraduate level. It states that there is too much 'spoon feeding' and 'teaching to the test' (Brannum, 2012). Such an approach would widen the gap between A-level and GCSE, and so it would be important to structure the qualifications students take at 16 years in a similar fashion to avoid this happening. Many 'skills' asked for by universities (Black and Lee, 2009) revolve around critical thinking, reflection, research skills, essay writing and independent learning, which can be instilled through a sound information literacy policy in schools, maybe even down to primary level.

The IBO expects a qualified librarian to play a role in delivering these skills. At Box Hill School, I have considerable input at sixth form level into many parts of the IB Diploma. A general introduction to the library and a brief demonstration of the subscription online databases are given in the first-year induction session. All students are signed up to Surrey Libraries and we have access to local university libraries at Guildford and Kingston. A corporate membership of the London Library gives access to further print and online material, including databases, such as JSTOR. Use of these resources is pushed through individual research-based lessons using joint classroom delivery followed by library research with corresponding documentation.

My approach to teaching

As Librarian, my role is to ease the progression from school to higher education by giving students the tools they need to become information literate. Many schools view the librarian's core role as encouraging and promoting the reading of fiction. While this is undoubtedly important, my belief is that teaching information-handling skills should take precedence, since the librarian is often the sole member of staff able to deliver this important life skill.

The majority of my lessons involve collaborative team-teaching with a subject specialist. The information literacy element is embedded in the overall lesson plan rather than being a discrete element. A key contributor to the success we have achieved in adopting the approach of the ANCIL strands has been my involvement in assessment. I have ensured that information literacy is given equal value to subject knowledge. For example, we reward students who show reflective, critical learning and who demonstrate they can construct an argument. Extra marks can be gained if they use resources beyond Google and Wikipedia and even for using a presentation format other than PowerPoint. The lessons outlined next in this chapter illustrate this approach to learning.

Introducing the library: Years 7 and 8 – Key Stage 3 (11–12+ years)

The youngest students arrive at Box Hill School from a variety of primary and preparatory schools. Many feeder schools do not have a formal library (Brennan, 2010). With busy working parents, students may be unfamiliar with public libraries too (Goulding, 2006). The initial library induction is designed to be a fun introduction to what is available.

In the autumn term induction session, I explain to students there has been a disaster and the library leaflets have all been destroyed by accident. I ask for help in designing a new one to show what we have in the library. For 30 minutes they look around and add ideas to their leaflet. My assistant, teaching colleagues and I act as prompts. In a plenary we review the leaflets and decide with the students which ones would give the best overview of the library (carefully making sure all the leaflets are commended for something).

This exercise is useful on several levels:

1   It allows both form teachers and me to gauge prior knowledge of libraries and experience of finding information.
2   It permits students to touch and explore the resources.
3   It encourages students to ask questions and interact with adults in their quest for information.
4   It encourages an independent approach to learning.

The main library induction occurs two weeks into the term, allowing time for students to settle in, having been set homework. Five one-hour dedicated lessons are conducted through English and Personal Social Health Education (PSHE) slots. Some classes may get two lessons a week. The course is short and snappy. PHSE covers 'emotions' and so library lessons are themed around 'happiness' to engender good feelings about our department. The lessons promote an understanding of the different resources on offer, organization, and independent thought and decision making.

Lesson 1 (fiction)

This coincides with Book Trust's 'Booked Up' scheme, offering free books to Year 7 (replaced in 2012 by a subsidised scheme, 'Bookbuzz' – see www.booktrust.org.uk). We describe the titles on offer and lead a discussion about the features of fiction books and reading choice. The lesson also considers arrangements of fiction books. Each student is given a paper 'bookworm' who has a liking for a specified genre. Students have to find a book they think their worm might like to read in order to feel happy, and explain why to the class.

Lesson 2 (reference)

Here we explore encyclopedias, dictionaries and thesauruses. I show different types of reference books and we debate the merits of finding this information online, via an app or in print form. In particular, the advantages and disadvantages of Wikipedia are discussed. A dictionary exercise involves pairs of students making a word web beginning with the word 'happy'. This is placed centrally on the paper. One student looks up 'happy' using a dictionary and finds an alternative word. A link is drawn to it. The paired student looks up this new word to find an alternative and so it continues until a web is formed. This gives students confidence in using dictionaries, alphabetical order and spotting unusual links between words and concepts (qualities very much needed for independent learning and critical thinking).

Lesson 3 (non-fiction)

Students are introduced to Dewey Classification. We begin with a 'Tower of Information' game (Pavey, 2006) whereby the students are assigned to be caretakers of a floor corresponding to a Dewey series. For example the reference section is manned by a 'Know All' in reception and the 'Boffin' resides on Level 5. Later, we put into practice what has been learned with a lateral thinking exercise (Pavey, 2006). This lesson gives some basic organizational information to aid independent learning followed by encouragement of independent thought, critical thinking and decision making.

Lesson 4 (selection)

The penultimate lesson comprises a team quiz. Groups have a set of four questions and four books. The questions are designed to test different ways of searching for information. One is factual, requiring the index; another is in a book where the answer is found via the contents page; the third necessitates the reader skimming through the book for the answer; and the final question involves the reader in making up their own mind, e.g. a book of party cakes with the question 'Which cake would you be happiest to receive?'. After ten minutes there is a table swap and this occurs twice more. A plenary allows discussion on how challenging the students found the exercise and why.

Lesson 5 (synthesis)

Finally, the students create their own poster for an alien to describe the concept of 'happiness'. Each has to contain a quote from a fiction book, a non-fiction book and a reference book with a bibliography. This introduces recording where information has come from and choosing suitable quotes. We use the posters in displays.

Library induction lessons are deliberately biased towards print resources, being the medium least familiar to our students. However, work continues with projects where research involves use of the library. Such lessons begin with team teaching alongside the subject teacher in the classroom. A resource box is set up and this is taken to the classroom where I can introduce students to appropriate websites and mobile apps. A research guide is added to the library catalogue and also to the library Netvibes pages (www.netvibes.com/ boxhillschool).

Additionally, in collaboration with the science department, we decided to try and teach students in Year 8 to research and compose a short Diploma-style essay using a mind map planning approach. We presented our interim findings at the LILAC 2012 conference (Pavey and Monk, 2012).

Project-based work and classroom topics: Years 9 to 11 – Key Stage 3/4 (13–16+ years)

Year 9 is the final period before students begin the GCSE syllabus. It is students in Year 9 who gain most experience in using the library for project-based work. Teachers work with me as Librarian to introduce the topic in the classroom and then to research in the library. I am very insistent that I am included in the outcome of this work and have a formal role in assessment.

In the module 'African Music' the teacher and I decided that, instead of using PowerPoint, we would ask the students to prepare a podcast. Each student was given a different African country to research, comparing and contrasting traditional and modern music. I explained the book resources on offer, demonstrated online information sources on the topic and led a discussion on 'what makes an effective podcast'. I prepared information sheets for the research and on making a podcast. Both the teacher and I marked the final work. The teacher awarded points for content and music technology and I gave marks for presentation, referencing, evidence of critical thinking and organization of information.

This approach gives the students an understanding that copy and paste will not gain the best grades. When peer marking is added to the process students are quick to spot presentations without all of the required elements. Students can understand the need to synthesize their own interpretation of their research – a vital quality for higher education.

With our GCSE students, we are aware that any involvement of the library has to be beneficial to the examination course if it is to be taken seriously by students. Opportunities are limited. In some subjects such as design technology there is a paper including a research element. In 2012 this involved designing a small container in the style of Charles Rennie Mackintosh. I conducted a lesson with the teacher explaining the available resources in print and online and set up supporting documents, catalogue entries and a Netvibes page. I explained the importance of demonstrating to the examiner that students had carried out their own research. It is this synthesis that proves so difficult for students, especially because GCSE courses generally expect students to regurgitate facts rather than use facts to express original thoughts. Teachers, too, are unused to handling independent learning research in this way.

Through PHSE, I collaborate to produce a two-lesson programme covering use of the internet and media. The purpose is to keep an interest in information literacy with the emphasis on this being a life skill rather than something to be learned for an examination. For Year 9, I devised a lesson to fit in with a module on friendship entitled 'Celebrity Best Friend'. This required students to research a definition of friendship, examples of ideals of friendship, and qualities their best friend had. Students picked a celebrity and decided what best friend qualities they had. Referencing of sources was obligatory. Finally, they created an avatar for the person (celebrity or current best friend) that they would choose as their best friend and revealed the answer by creating a QR Code.

In Year 10 the PHSE module looks at the internet versus print as an information source. I use a co-operative learning technique. Students are divided into groups of four and given a research question relating to climate change. Two students form an argument for using print resources and two promote using the internet. They each argue with one person on the opposite side and then again with the alternative pair until a group consensus is formed of how they would conduct their research. This is read to the class who debate the findings. A discussion follows on how much trust we can place on information sources and an analysis of web addresses and domain names. The lessons cover spoof websites and alternative search engines to Google, Yahoo! and Bing.

Through another exercise I emphasize the importance of choosing the right keywords for searching. One student has their back to a screen showing a picture and a word and the class give this student one-word clues without giving away the actual word. The clues are written on a board and once the word is guessed correctly we discuss whether the other words could have been used to retrieve the needed information. We begin with easy words such as 'car' and 'horse', then progress to concepts such as 'gentleman' and 'resistance'.

Developing reflective and critical thinking – Pre-IB Diploma and Sixth Form (16–18+ years)

The demands of the IB Diploma are very different from those for A-level. Students are rewarded for reflective and critical thinking and for research skills. This is assessed through the Theory of Knowledge course and the Extended Essay, both of which need to be passed at Grade D minimum to gain the Diploma. It is not optional.

Theory of Knowledge is based upon philosophy and questions where knowledge originates. It occurs in every subject of the IB and is also a course in its own right. It is assessed through group presentation and a 1500-word essay. The assessment attempts to judge how well the student can form an argument and debate it to a conclusion using factual information and/or personal experience to support their claims.

The Extended Essay is a 4000-word academic essay. The research topic of choice is drawn from a subject the student is taking and wants to explore further. The essay needs to demonstrate writing and referencing in an academic style. The content has to be reflective, using the research to uphold any points made. Even when the essay is in a practical subject such as chemistry, marks are awarded for the analysis and interpretation of the results rather than on the technical skill of the experiment. Furthermore, all internal assessments gain marks for correct academic presentation.

Intense tuition in information skills is given at timely and relevant intervals in the Extended Essay journey:

Session 1

Rationale of the Extended Essay, research and evaluation of findings. This covers the mark scheme. Information sheets giving specific details of the requirements within each subject are given to students.

Session 2

Question formation. Ideally students' research is planned around a question. The student, supervisor and I look at the feasibility with regard to available resources.

Session 3

Research. Students complete an essay jigsaw (Pavey, 2011) demonstrating the emotions they may experience in research and write up, e.g. their frustrations, deadlines and elation on completion. Most students will not have written such a lengthy piece of work before. The exercise addresses plagiarism and keeping track of references. In subject-specific groups students are taken through useful databases in more depth. Using the mind map approach outlined earlier and with encouragement to use programs such as Microsoft OneNote or Evernote they plan their essay and begin research.

Session 4

Writing up. Students are given individual guidance on referencing, a style guide, booklets and video links via the Netvibes pages and the catalogue. They use a library checklist to ensure they have the correct emphasis on critical evaluation rather than narrative. Subject content is reviewed by their supervisor.

Session 5

Once the essay is at final draft stage it is put through Turnitin (www.turnitin. com), a plagiarism detection programme. This is used as a teaching tool so that the student can see how their referenced quotations have been found and to highlight areas where they might have paraphrased or missed a reference.

Some sessions run over several days, when students are 'off timetable', giving them time to complete them. These have been fine-tuned and, together with the IB Co-ordinator, we have amended the content and adjusted the timings. We plan to run Session 3 as a series of optional seminars on different databases plus an appointments surgery for one-to-one consultation.

Conclusion

Overall, teaching information skills at Box Hill School is embedded into some part of the curriculum in every year group. It does not adhere to any strict model, as summarized by Bond (2011), but tends to be needs-driven. The concept of using information literacy to enhance intrinsic motivation is an exciting move that we will explore further.

I am fortunate in having a very supportive senior management team and to work with inspiring, creative and experimental teachers. Many school librarians do not have this opportunity – either because they work alone (and working hours reduce their job to a functional level only), or because they work in schools where teaching to the test is a priority. Increasingly, many secondary schools are closing their library and making the librarian redundant, while others are choosing to replace Chartered librarians with unqualified staff. At Box Hill School we endeavour to develop and teach our students the information-handling skills they need throughout their school career to give them the best start at university. How will students from other establishments meet the demands of higher education with regard to expectations of information and digital literacy?

Bibliography

Bartlett, J. and Miller, C. (2011) *Truth, Lies and the Internet: a report into young people's digital fluency, Demos,* www.demos.co.uk/publications/truth-lies-and-the-internet.

Black, F. and Lee, S. (2009) *Staff Ratings: required skills on arrival at university,* Mission Ambition Russell Group Conference, May. Cited in: Fuller, C. (2011) *Bridging the Gap: the skills gap between FE and HE, and what can be done to reduce it,* PowerPoint, Assessment and Qualifications Alliance, http://store.aqa.org.uk/support/pdf/AQA-W-SIXFORM-BRIDGING-THE-GAP.PPT.

Bond, T. (2011) *Information Literacy Models and Inquiry Learning Models,* http://ictnz.com/infolitmodels.htm.

Brennan, G. (2010) Book Smart: why every primary pupil needs a library, *Independent*, 18 February, www.independent.co.uk/news/education/schools/book-smart-why-every-primary-pupil-needs-a-library-1902376.html.

Goulding, A (2006) *Public Libraries in the 21st Century*, Ashgate Publishing.

Herring, J. (2009) *A Grounded Analysis of Year 8 Students' Reflections on Information Literacy Skills and Technique*, International Association of School Librarianship, www.iasl-online.org/pubs/slw/jan09-herring.htm.

Higher Education Institutions: how do they fare? (2011) International Baccalaurate Organisation, www.ibo.org/research/programmevalidation/documents/HESAResearchSummary_Final.pdf.

Higher Education Statistics Agency (2011) *International Baccalaureate Students Studying at UK*.

International Baccalaureate Organisation (2004) *Implementing the IB Diploma Programme*, Cambridge University Press, http://assets.cambridge.org/97805215/44870/sample/9780521544870ws.pdf.

Murdock, T. B. and Anderman, E. M. (2006) Motivational Approaches to Classroom Cheating: towards an integrated model of academic dishonesty, *Educational Psychologist*, **41**, 129–45.

Pavey, S. (2006) *Information Literacy Games for Schools*, www.lilacconference.com/dw/archive/resources/2006/PaveyS.ppt.

Pavey, S. (2011) *Jigsaws: a first step to academic essay-writing in schools*, www.youtube.com/watch?v=P1kCzufnTZc.

Pavey, S. and Monk, R. (2012) *Catch Them Early: information literacy based assessment for learning with Year 8 at Box Hill School*, PowerPoint, www.slideshare.net/infolit_group/pavey-monk.

Stratton, A. (2012) *Michael Gove Wants Universities to Create New A-levels*, www.bbc.co.uk/news/education-17588292.

Strand Two

Becoming an independent learner

Geoff Walton and Jamie Cleland

Strand Two is informed by the belief that change occurs throughout the learning process as a natural, inevitable and sometimes challenging aspect of learning. Building on the transitional issues identified in Strand One, Strand Two positions the concept of 'learning to learn' as a lifelong framework for encountering, evaluating and assimilating new information, including evidence that conflicts with or challenges the learner's beliefs and world view.

The concept of the autonomous learner is fundamental to this vision. Rather than endeavouring to teach students how to deal with every kind of information, this strand aims to facilitate their emergence as individuals capable of generating strategies for dealing with new information contexts as required, at every stage in their lives.

Geoff is a well known researcher and practitioner in the information literacy field, and a member of the RIN Working Group on Information Literacy. He has written and published widely in the field as well as conducting doctoral research, and took part in the ANCIL expert consultation.

We are delighted that Geoff's colleague Jamie Cleland, a senior lecturer in Sport Sociology at Staffordshire University, has co-authored this chapter, making it an outstanding example of interprofessional collaboration.

Institutional context and module development (Geoff)

This chapter will draw upon six years' work carried out in collaboration with academic colleagues in Sport and Exercise Science at Staffordshire University, especially Dr Jamie Cleland, who also contributes to this chapter. The specific focus is a core first-year module called Research and Professional Development (between 120 and 160 per cohort). Before the module leader and I became involved in this particular module it was notoriously unpopular amongst students, who found it boring, unnecessary and full of material they 'knew already' because they had 'done it all at college'. Yet these students, who, according to their own informal self-assessment, seemed to have arrived at university with a complete set of study skills and with claims that suggested they were at the highest levels of information literacy, produced essays and other assignments that told a very different story.

It is perhaps unsurprising that the narrative from the module leader and his team was one of frustration: students produced essays with poor sentence structure, could not argue effectively, and used inadequate, often internet-based resources found via the first page of a two-keyword Google search. In effect, students would exit the module with a set of less than effective lifelong learning skills and a low level of information literacy. Coupled with this was a reticence to engage in class-based discussion and work collaboratively. In short, neither students nor academics liked being involved in it, students' grades were mediocre and there was plenty of scope for a rethink.

The teaching and learning programme that Jamie and I developed has produced a number of far-reaching impacts since its implementation in 2007–8. The changes in the pedagogic approach to the module have had a positive impact on learners' assessed work, transferable skills, approaches to learning and approaches to essay writing.

Overview of updated module content (Jamie)

The module described here (and outlined in Table 2.1) was developed after many planning meetings between Geoff and me and has now been in operation for six years. The 'study skills' elements and subject strands were developed by me, and Geoff devised the information literacy components and the online peer assessment intervention. The programme fosters learning skills in students and encourages them to think critically, reflect, communicate and collaborate through regular practice.

The module consists of four main phases of learning. In the first phase, which takes place during induction week, students answer a question and write a 500-word essay which they submit at the end of that week. The essay question for the 2009/10 cohort was 'What defines success in sport?', a

Table 2.1 *The module programme (information literacy elements in bold)*

Week	Lecture	Workshop
1	Introduction to the Module	Reflecting on the Essay Process
2	Learning and Teaching in Higher Education	Learning Styles
3	**Developing Research Skills**	**Using e-Resources**
4	**Plagiarism and Referencing**	**Internet-based session**
5	**Writing Styles (1): The written word**	**Understanding Plagiarism and Referencing**
6	**Writing Styles (2): Report writing, reading and summarizing**	**Online Peer Assessment: essay introduction**
7	**Assessment, Feedback and Revision**	**Online Peer Assessment: essay main body**
8	**Introduction to Qualitative Research**	**Online Peer Assessment: essay conclusion and bibliography**
9	Introduction to Quantitative Research	Qualitative Methodologies – choosing the right methodology
10	Qualitative Research (2)	Quantitative Methodologies – becoming acquainted with statistical concepts
11	Quantitative Research (2)	Working with Qualitative / Quantitative data
12	Module Summary	Working with Qualitative / Quantitative data

deliberately open-ended, inquiry-based approach informed by the 'pedagogy of the question' (Andretta, 2006). For example, a sport therapy student might define success as rehabilitating an injured athlete back to fitness whereas a sport development student might see success in working with a disadvantaged group of people. The essay is formatively assessed by personal tutors and fed back face-to-face within one week.

The second phase occurs during the early part of the module, where key skills in effective learning in higher education (including essay writing, information literacy – research, critical thinking, plagiarism and referencing – note-taking and summarizing) are taught, all focusing on the inquiry-based question already given to the students. The idea is to build up to the end of week 5, when the students have another opportunity to hand in an 800-word version of the same question, this time formatively peer-assessed on Blackboard, the virtual learning environment (VLE) employed at Staffordshire University.

The third phase incorporates aspects of Staffordshire University's online Assignment Survival Kit (ASK)[1] and concentrates on academic weeks 6–8, when the students participate in online peer assessment in their tutor group. Each group consists of up to 20 students who provide reciprocal feedback on aspects of one another's work on a weekly basis. The structure of this three-week programme is:

- Week 6 – essay introduction
- Week 7 – essay main body
- Week 8 – essay conclusion and referencing style.

During the peer assessment task students are directed to the ASK section on essay construction, which forms the basis for feedback during each peer assessment workshop. Each student provides a weekly qualitative online analysis of each section of their peer's formative submission. The notion of 'scaffolding' is introduced here, with a set of instructions provided for the first workshop and more autonomy given by the third workshop (Mayes and de Freitas, 2007). Although no grade is given during this exercise, the students are made aware of the grading criteria adopted and how a piece of work is assessed.

Here, students begin to learn the three stages of assessment adopted by Biggs at an early stage of their degree programme (Biggs, 2003, 161):

1   *setting the criteria* for assessing work
2   *selecting the evidence* that would be relevant to submit to judgement against those criteria
3   *making a judgement* about the extent to which these criteria have been met.

Biggs suggests that students need to learn the assessment criteria and apply it to themselves. This, he argues, is beneficial, as they learn whether a piece of work meets the given criteria. It has been suggested that this helps develop a student's ability and provides them with an opportunity to authenticate and exploit data and information for their own educational benefit and that of their peers; in short to become 'students as scholars' (Hodge et al., 2008, 5–6).

Once this iterative practice is completed, students then undertake the fourth phase (review and amend) and submit a summative 1500-word version of the same essay question in week 12. We argue that new and innovative ways of engaging students through assessment are needed (see also Bostock and Street, 2011). This chapter concentrates on the combination of enquiry-based learning, information literacy and e-learning and how they are built into an online peer assessment exercise. What we shall present is that this learning strategy has positive benefits to student learning. Thus, and in contrast to Topping's (1998) scepticism regarding the actual benefits of self- and peer assessment, this chapter suggests that a well embedded and structured online peer assessment exercise provides many long-term benefits to student learning.

The beauty of the learning and teaching approach of which this e-learning element is a part is that because it is eclectic – it uses workshops, discussions, online discussions, lectures, mini-lectures, seminars and small group work – it covers all learner preferences, making it an effective way of delivering learning. The approach also supports the development of transferable skills, particularly searching effectively for information to back up an argument, evaluating it thoroughly, referencing it properly – both in text and in a bibliography – redrafting of essays, and working collaboratively with peers. Tutors reported that students did appear to transfer these skills to other modules.

Tutors also noted that students had formerly seemed to hand in their first draft, because the written work tended to be riddled with typos, lacked references, arguments were not coherent and a logical structure was lacking. Evidence from focus group interviews carried out in 2010 revealed that, since the new intervention, students were re-drafting their essays at least once, some up to six or seven times before handing them in.

To test the statistical significance of the grades obtained in week 1 and week 12, an independent samples test was conducted between the two sets of grades for two tutor groups chosen at random. The test indicated that there had a significant improvement in students' performance on the two assignments.

E-learning elements (Geoff and Jamie)

Mayes and de Freitas (2007) argue that scaffolding – a process by which skills, rules and knowledge involved in learning are internalized – creates the cognitive tools to enable self-directed learning. It does this by allowing the locus of control to pass from the tutor to increasingly competent learners, so that the learner becomes able to do alone what formerly s/he could only do in collaboration with the tutor.

In tandem with this is a need by the tutor to understand how communities form (especially student learning communities), usually because they identify with something such as a need, a common shared goal and identity. In this sense the social dimension is critical to learning, even, somewhat counter-intuitively, independent learning. Translating this to the e-learning context is critical in constructing e-learning opportunities. The model used to structure these ideas into a coherent online learning and teaching intervention is based on recommendations by Goodyear (2001) and his classification of courseware:

1   'Primary courseware' is used to convey information, such as online lecture notes and reading lists (i.e. subject matter).
2   'Secondary courseware' is used to question and encourage reflection in students (i.e. the Assignment Survival Kit – ASK).
3   'Tertiary courseware' enables the production of materials by previous and current learners in the course of discussing and assessing their learning (i.e. online peer discussion).

In effect, tertiary courseware creates a 'cognitive space' (Garrison, Anderson and Garrison, 2003) or time to think, where students can give a far more considered reply online than in the immediacy and ephemeral context of a face-to-face conversation. Walton and Hepworth's (2011) empirical study corroborates this theory, finding that a greater learning effect was noted in those students who experience tertiary courseware than in those who experience primary or secondary courseware only.

By using all three levels of courseware and scaffolding, a rich, motivating and engaging learning experience ensues. To make this so, the online learning and teaching segment of the intervention contained procedural information on how to perform the activities (primary courseware – a Word document), online resources that students could interact with (secondary courseware – the online tool, the Assignment Survival Kit) and finally online discourse via the Blackboard VLE (tertiary courseware). Using these three levels of courseware together creates an effective online environment that encourages the online discourse on which the online peer assessment is based.

Online peer assessment activity (Jamie and Geoff)

Not surprisingly a number of students were apprehensive about the peer assessment exercise, as most had not engaged in such an activity before. However, when they were asked subsequently what it meant for them, a large number of students stressed that it had the potential to impact positively on their future learning. Here are just a few examples of the feedback and anxiety themes to which students regularly referred in the initial survey:

Feedback

It's a really good idea, hearing everyone's different comments to improve. Effective feedback will help me know where I went wrong. It is good as we're all communicating with each other giving positive feedback and effective criticism to help improve.

(Student 15)

I'm looking for a much wider range of constructive criticism to help improve my writing style and learning process (research, referencing etc.) for future modules.

(Student 91)

Anxiety

Nervous that I won't meet the standards of others and my assessment will be negative. I'll be a bit defensive at first but will learn that we are all in the same situation.

(Student 33)

Slightly apprehensive but intrigued as to the different opinions that may occur through this exercise.

(Student 95)

Despite their initial apprehension about this exercise, 90% of students who responded to the questionnaire indicated that the online peer assessment exercise had been worthwhile and aided their learning. This may be due to the scaffolded approach discussed earlier, which enabled students to demonstrate greater independence in their feedback and reflection. Indeed, despite their initial scepticism of the exercise some students seemed to change their opinion once it had been completed:

> At first I wasn't 100 percent comfortable but I then discovered that it was really beneficial to my learning. This whole process helped my understanding of essay writing and the ways in which I can improve.
>
> (Student 74)

> Better than I thought. Really helpful as I got a range of feedback from different people. It also benefitted me reading my peers' work and seeing how they write.
>
> (Student 95)

During this survey, the most regularly used comments were 'helpful' and 'useful', indicating that students thought it a beneficial exercise.

Traditional assessment methods often encourage surface learning. In trying to encourage a deeper approach, an increasing range of formative assessment opportunities has been suggested and discussed. The most interesting by far to us is the work on peer assessment in education and how it can help students form judgements about high-quality work (see Bostock, 2000; Boud, 1995). The learning environment continues to move from individualized to self-directed and collaborative learning, and Brown et al. (2009) and Orsmond and Merry (1996) show how this learning environment has gradually changed from being purely tutor-assessed to one in which students are frequently involved in the assessment of each other. Given this change in assessment strategy, Boud, Cohen and Sampson (1999) remark that peer assessment fits perfectly with the desired outcomes of self-directed, peer and ultimately independent learning.

Peer assessment empowers students as learners, motivating them to collaborate with one another and to begin to develop themselves as autonomous learners. Orsmond, Merry and Callaghan (2004) suggest that peer assessment provides students with an opportunity to demonstrate many key transferrable skills such as responsibility, collaboration, discussion and reflection, all of which are important skills, which should be enhanced during an undergraduate programme.

Finally, the effectiveness of any form of assessment depends on its quality and how each student incorporates it in their learning. For a peer assessment exercise such as this to work and enhance student learning, the quality of feedback given by students to one another is crucial. We shall let the students speak for themselves below.

Impact (Geoff and Jamie)

The online peer assessment exercise, as evidenced by the online discourse, appeared to sensitize students to information literacy issues in a way that a straightforward face-to-face approach might not. Here it can be seen that students, through their comments to others about their work, reveal a high order of information discernment:

. . . try to use academic references instead of autobiographies. (Student A)

Your whole reference list are [sic] websites. Could you know [sic] use books as it's easier as you don't have to worry if they are credible? (Student B)

. . . include more [sources] that are more up-to-date. (Student C)

. . . could use references from books as well as the internet. (Student D)

I like the use of historical references as well as up to date ones on this. Interesting stuff too. (Student E)

A good use of quotes throughout from good sources e.g. the NHS . . . (Student F)

Also, your quote from the Guardian. They didn't find that out, they are commenting on what others have researched so just be careful how you word it. (Student G)

This clearly demonstrates that students, as independent learners, are beginning to get to grips with information discernment and are able to make quality judgements about the information their peers are using or not using. This in turn shows that the students making the comments have gained a sophisticated idea of specific evaluation criteria: they are coming to terms with the differences between good-quality research and other sources (students A, B, D, F and G), and the notion of currency (Students C and E) and historical value (student E).

Pedagogic principles (Geoff)

The need to be information literate is generally agreed: the difficult part is in characterizing information literacy in a meaningful, theoretically and empirically grounded way so that it can be successfully delivered in the teaching and learning environment.

Information literacy is not a subject per se but a thinking skills framework that empowers learners to engage with information of any kind. It is highly context-specific and must be woven into the fabric of the subject being taught. The models of information literacy in existence all share a set of core characteristics, which focus on the complex set of skills learners need to find, evaluate and use information appropriately (Walton, 2009). It is also very clear from research into inquiry-based learning that for information literacy interventions to be successful they require a shift from teaching specific resources to facilitating the ability to use a set of critical thinking skills to engage with information. Therefore, information literacy is a fundamental building block of inquiry-based approaches – an argument corroborated by Levy and Petrulis (2007).

Some readers may remember my presentation at the Librarians' Information Literacy Annual Conference (LILAC) in 2010 where I 'demolished' the Seven Pillars (Walton, 2010). Here, for the first time in print, is the 'wrecking ball', which is the empirically grounded theoretical definition and model presented at LILAC. Learning involves many things: a context such as a university which provides a framework of roles, e.g. student and tutor, and associated norms, such as attending seminars and completing assignments; cognitive processes, such as thinking about something and possibly analysing and applying it; thinking about that analysis – reflection or metacognition; having feelings about the process, such as anxiety; and possibly changing behaviour as a result of all this, for example being able to make balanced judgements about a piece of information and use it appropriately in a given context.

In a nutshell, here is the new theory of information literacy which underpins my approach.

Becoming information literate appears to be about an individual completing a task in a given context (this context frames their roles and norms, e.g. a student required to complete an assignment). This context leads to the interaction with sources (e.g. databases, e-journals, books, e-books, peers, tutors and other individuals) and in so doing brings about the interplay of an individual's behavioural, cognitive, metacognitive and affective states. It is this interplay that determines the level of new knowledge learnt (or produced, or both) and the degree of changed behaviour (i.e. level of information literacy) exhibited.

This can be expressed diagrammatically as the three spheres of information literacy (Figure 2.1).

My own view is that each sphere is intertwined with the others, and each becomes more or less important at certain times in the process. However, my overarching argument would be that unless one has some idea or template of what good information looks like to start with, one is unlikely to be able to find and use similar information in the future. In other words, being able to discern good information from bad is at the very heart of becoming information literate.

How does this theory align with the ANCIL model? Like ANCIL, it is a

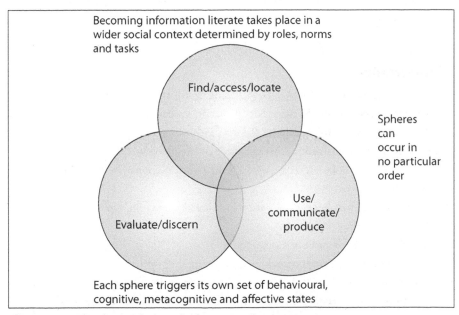

Figure 2.1 *The three spheres of information literacy*

holistic model where the learner is at the centre of the process and the experience is seen as social rather than solely individual. There is a strong emphasis on subject context, skills and learning as a continuous journey. The creation of new knowledge, which includes information-handling skills, is also emphasized.

The learning and teaching intervention discussed above fits the ANCIL Strand Two criteria by developing practical skills and a subject context (see module programme, Table 2.1 above) within which students deploy the skills; and high-level cognitive operations including critical evaluation, synthesis and creating new knowledge (see online peer assessment discourse), culminating in the conscious, reflective framework (see questionnaire responses and online peer assessment) that is key to managing their own learning.

Notes

1   ASK is software specifically for undergraduates, which provides an information-literacy thinking skills framework for completing assignments (Adams, Pope and Walton, 2008). Students type in their assignment deadline and ASK calculates the stages (and by when) students should undertake assignment tasks such as: planning; finding, evaluating and using information; and note-taking and referencing.

Bibliography

Adams, J. Pope, A. and Walton, G. (2008) Using Web 2.0 to Enhance the Staffordshire University Assignment Survival Kit (ASK). In Parker, J. E. and Godwin, P. (eds), *Information Literacy Meets Library 2.0*, Facet Publishing.

Andretta, S. (2006) Information Literacy: the new 'pedagogy of the question'. In Walton, G. and Pope, A. (eds), *Information Literacy: recognising the need,* Chandos Publishing.

Biggs, J. (2003) *Teaching for Quality Learning at University*, 2nd edn, Open University Press.

Bostock, S. (2000) Student Peer Assessment, www.keele.org.uk/docs/bostock_peer_assessment.htm.

Bostock, S. and Street, M. (2011) Modelling Assessment Processes across a University and Introducing Technology-based Innovations, www.keele.org.uk/docs/059%20SB-MW%20ICICTE%20article%20March2011v6.pdf.

Boud, D. (1995) *Enhancing Learning Through Self-Assessment*, Kogan Page.

Boud, D., Cohen, R. and Sampson, J. (1999) Peer Learning and Assessment, *Assessment and Evaluation in Higher Education*, **24**, 413–26.

Brown, G. T. L., Irving, S. E., Peterson, E. R. and Hirschfield, G. H. F. (2009) Use of Interactive-informal Assessment Practices: New Zealand secondary students' conceptions of assessment, *Learning and Instruction*, **19**, 97–111.

Garrison, D. R., Anderson, T. and Garrison, R. (2003) *E-learning in the 21st Century: a framework for research and practice*, Routledge.

Goodyear, P. (2001) *Effective Networked Learning in Higher Education: notes and guidelines, Networked Learning in Higher Education Project: JISC Committee for Awareness Liaison and Training (JCALT)*, Volume 3 of the final report to JCALT. http://usyd.academia.edu/PeterGoodyear/Books/269593/Effective_networked_ learning_in_higher_education_notes_and_guidelines.

Hodge, D., Haynes, C., Le Pore, P., Pasquesi, K. and Hirsh, M. (2008) From Inquiry to Discovery: developing the student as scholar in a networked world. In *Learning through Enquiry Alliance (LTEA) Conference, 25–27 June, University of Sheffield*, http://cilass-resources.group.shef.ac.uk/ltea2008/Hodge_CETL_2008_ keynote.pdf.

Levy, P. and Petrulis, R. (2007) Towards Transformation? First year students, inquiry-based learning and the research/teaching nexus. In: *Proceedings of the Annual Conference of the Society for Research into Higher Education (SRHE), 11–13 December 2007, Brighton, UK*.

Mayes, T. and de Freitas, S. (2007) Learning and E-learning: the role of theory. In Beetham, H. and Sharpe, R. (eds), *Rethinking Pedagogy for a Digital Age: designing and delivering e-learning*, Routledge.

Orsmond, P. and Merry, S. (1996) The Importance of Marking Criteria in the Use of Peer Assessment, *Assessment and Evaluation in Higher Education*, **21**, 239–50.

Orsmond, P., Merry, S. and Callaghan, A. (2004) Implementation of a Formative Assessment Model Incorporating Peer and Self-assessment, *Innovations in Education and Teaching International*, 41, 273–90.

Topping, K. J. (1998) Peer Assessment between Students in Colleges and Universities, *Review of Educational Research*, **68**, 249–76.

Walton, G. (2009) *Developing a New Blended Approach to Fostering Information Literacy*, unpublished PhD thesis, Loughborough University.

Walton, G. (2010) Demolishing the Seven Pillars: a warning from research?, www.lilacconference.com/dw/programme/Presentations/Tuesday/City_View_S uite/Walton_Demolishing.pdf.

Walton, G. and Hepworth, M. (2011) A Longitudinal Study of Changes in Learners' Cognitive States During and Following an Information Literacy Teaching Intervention, *Journal of Documentation*, **67** (3), 449–79.

Strand Three

Developing academic literacies

Moira Bent

Strand Three aims to articulate, explore and develop the academic literacies of reading and writing in line with ANCIL's view of information literacy as a continuum ranging from functional skills through to high-level intellectual operations. The content of this strand therefore embraces not only key skills and strategies in academic reading and writing, such as skimming and scanning strategies and recognizing and using appropriate academic idiom, but also higher-order contextual activities such as textual interrogation and critiquing, argument construction, and understanding of a discipline's epistemological structure and values.

Moira has made a significant contribution to information literacy not only in the UK but internationally. She is a member of the SCONUL working group for information literacy, which recently launched an updated version of the 'Seven Pillars' model, is an experienced practitioner and has written and presented widely on information literacy. She is also a National Teaching Fellow and took part in the ANCIL expert consultation. Here she describes a staff training and support initiative which illustrates how closely academic literacies and information literacy are interrelated.

Institutional context

This case study describes a project designed to provide opportunities for teaching staff to embed information literacy concepts into the curriculum in Newcastle University, UK, and in Newcastle University in Singapore (NUIS). Developed from an existing methodology to appreciate information literacy within the context of academic literacies, the work builds on and extends several previous and concurrent initiatives.

Newcastle University, a Russell Group University located in the north-east of England, has 21,000 students, of whom 6000 are postgraduates, 4000 are international and a growing number are learning at a distance from the main campus. In common with many other universities, examples of best practice in developing academic literacies can be found alongside much less developed practice (Bent and Stockdale, 2009). Information literacy is recognized at a strategic level in the university: as digital literacy in the strategic plan, within the Graduate Skills framework and more explicitly in the e-portfolio system which will be deployed across the institution in 2012. The e-portfolio will enable students to reflect on their learning and identify areas, including information literacy, in which they need to develop. However, while information literacy is included in the portfolio, the interpretation does focus mainly on skills aspects, as is to be expected. Module Outline Forms encourage teaching staff to indicate whether information literacy is introduced, practised or assessed in their module. In practice this is very much a paper exercise, although it does provide a mechanism for starting discussions about the place of information literacy in the curriculum. Promoting and developing information and digital literacies is also a strategic priority for the library service.

Pedagogical concepts

In much of the traditional educational literature, the term academic literacy refers purely to the development of students' reading and writing skills: how to write an essay or report or how to reference, for example. However, more recently this view that literacy relates to the acquisition of specific transferable skills has been challenged (Lea and Street, 1998; Wingate, 2006), with academic literacy described as a social and cultural practice, which varies depending on context (Lea, 2004). This perspective of academic literacy as a 'complex, socially situated set of meaning making practices' (Gourlay, 2009, 182) allows us to align it with the new SCONUL definition of information literacy:

> Information literate people will demonstrate an awareness of how they gather, use, synthesize, manage and create information and data in an ethical manner and will have the information skills to do so effectively
>
> SCONUL (2011)

and with ANCIL's broad vision of information literacy as a fundamental element of learning.

There are clear parallels and overlaps in the concepts and terminology, which are enormously helpful when initiating conversations between librarians and educationalists and we could enter a debate about which is the broader term. Is information literacy just one of a range of academic literacies, or, as academic literacies deal with making meaning from information, should we view information literacy as the broader concept? In reality, the distinction is merely semantic, the value lying in the recognition that information literacy is not a simple transferable skill in which students can be 'trained', but a much more integral part of the learning process which needs to be embedded in students' wider learning experiences.

In the context of academic literacies, information literacy can be thought of as a learning habit or disposition (Claxton and Carr, 2004) which facilitates interaction with information throughout an individual's learning life. Thinking dispositions, such as a tendency to explore alternative views, the tendency to wonder and probe, to seek connections and explanations, and to be reflective, correlate well with this approach and allow us to position information literacy within a broader educational context (Perkins, Jay and Tishman, 1993). It is also helpful to distinguish between learning styles, attitudes and habits:

> Learning styles, which are a reflection of an individual's personality and are usually an unconscious trait, are difficult to influence or change. They can be thought of as the way in which a learner receives, sorts, interacts and processes information. Learning attitudes are frequently a conscious trait and often depend on motivations. A person's attitude to their learning, their views on the value of learning and why they are learning is also often influenced by factors beyond the classroom. In contrast, a learning habit describes the way in which a person has learned to learn.
>
> Bent and Stockdale (2009)

Information literacy development targets students' learning habits, encouraging them to approach their use of information in a more coherent way.

Information literacy development at Newcastle

With these concepts in mind, the overall approach at Newcastle has always been to move away from standalone skills teaching or online skills modules and focus on embedding information literacy development within a subject context whenever possible. Newcastle University Library has a long history of delivering information literacy skills workshops to students as well as instigating a variety of information literacy projects and initiatives. While some workshops focus on specific skills, there is a growing recognition that a common understanding of information literacy by academic staff is central to integrating information literacy into the curriculum. If information literacy is perceived purely as a set of skills then the emphasis can be confined to training; however, if information literacy is accepted as an attitude to or habit of learning, then an educative approach is needed (Town, 2003). Education in information literacy engages the students in reflective practice, critical reading and thinking and argument construction, learning specific information skills together with an awareness of the wider information world, its place in their discipline and its relevance in their learning. In order to achieve this transition successfully, information literacy needs to be taught by academic staff as part of the discipline and not perceived by the students as a dispensable add-on.

This is not an easy aim to achieve and there are many issues involved. Librarians have embraced the teaching of information literacy as one of our raisons d'être; it takes up a perhaps disproportionate amount of our time and many of us enjoy the interaction with students. If we accept that it is the role of faculty to develop students' information literacy, what then is the role of library staff? In addition, while we are clearly equipped to deliver skills training, engaging in debate with students about the less tangible aspects of information literacy is a different, much more challenging, proposition. This approach is also dependent on academic staff engaging with the agenda and making space in their teaching to facilitate information literacy development on an ongoing basis, embedded within the curriculum, rather than, as can often be the case, sending their students for a 'library workshop'.

It became clear several years ago at Newcastle that the key was to engage the academic community and encourage teachers to take ownership of information literacy development.

The Newcastle Information Literacy Project

In 2006 the Newcastle Information Literacy Project aimed to develop a community of practice across the university, bringing together staff from all disciplines and levels who evinced an interest in information literacy development. Networking meetings facilitated discussions and led ultimately to the development of the Information Literacy Toolkit (Bent and Brettell, 2006). The project team developed a programme structure based on the original SCONUL Seven Pillars model (SCONUL, 1999), which enabled teaching staff, both academic and library, to develop threads of information literacy activities within their teaching.

The toolkit, which consists of a collection of teaching resources (PowerPoint slides, handouts, examples of practice, links to online resources), was created as a resource to support the educators. One of the original ideas behind the toolkit was to keep it fresh with contributions from teachers; as they used and adapted the resources it was hoped they would redeposit their updated version in the toolkit. In practice, however, the deposit process was overly complex and while we know the resources in it are consulted, it proved impossible to keep the toolkit up to date or to monitor actual use of the materials.

Certificate of Advanced Studies in Academic Practice and Newcastle Teaching Award

The Certificate of Advanced Studies in Academic Practice (CASAP) offers experienced academics the opportunity for accreditation of personal and professional development in their academic practice. It is accredited by the Higher Education Academy accredited and consists of two modules and associated coursework. Module 1, the Newcastle Teaching Award (NTA) is compulsory for newly appointed teachers with less than five years' teaching experience.

For several years library staff contributed information literacy elements to the programme, resulting in several information literacy course works and subsequent information literacy champions among the new teaching staff. A variety of different mechanisms for embedding information literacy into the teaching curriculum resulted, initiated by academic staff and often wholly owned and taught by them. In fact, library staff are not always aware that such integration is happening, as it is so embedded within the discipline. Sadly,

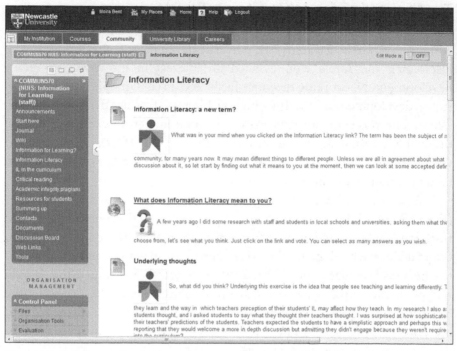

Figure 3.1   *Information for Learning: an online course for staff*

time constraints for the course curtailed the information literacy elements somewhat in recent years but they were revived in 2009 as part of a special CASAP Intensive programme for Nigerian lecturers. This programme, entitled 'Information for Learning', proved successful and has formed the basis for subsequent projects. Figure 3.1 shows part of the home page of the programme on the university website.

Information for Learning

The Information for Learning programme is run over two days and comprises a blend of practical information skills for staff underpinned by more discursive elements of information literacy. A sample programme is shown here:

CASAP Intensive: Aims of the sessions

During the Information for Learning programme we will:

- discuss our understanding of 'good academic conduct'
- think about how to integrate Information for Learning into our teaching
- use the Seven Pillars of Information Literacy model to develop curriculum content
- discuss critical reading in relation to developing information literacy
- investigate the drivers which influence students to plagiarize
- generate practical ways to minimize the likelihood of plagiarism occurring
- consider the Researcher Development Statement and its relevance to good academic conduct
- consider issues of culture and academic assumptions
- find out how we can better support students to develop their writing skills.

CASAP Intensive: Outcomes of the programme
After the Information for Learning programme participants should:

- have a clear understanding of the principles of good academic conduct
- have identified some key issues in supporting good academic conduct amongst students
- understand the relevance of Information for Learning in their teaching
- understand the importance of students developing the full range of information literacy skills to support learning beyond lectures
- have considered how information literacy development can be embedded into the curriculum
- know about some resources they can use to help integrate Information for Learning into their teaching
- have thought about culture and academic assumptions
- have identified ways to support students in writing.

Activities in the programme include discussions about the meaning of terms such as 'information' and 'good academic conduct' and participants are encouraged to discuss whether the various information literacy models are relevant to their teaching. Debates on issues such as plagiarism can become very animated and serve to demonstrate the relevance of an integrated information literacy approach across the curriculum. The sessions are supported by the resources in the Information Literacy Toolkit, and participants are also directed to Jorum (www.jorum.ac.uk) and other quality information literacy resources. Feedback from participants has been positive:

the Information for Learning was the most interesting part of the course

I hadn't heard of information literacy before. Now I need to think about what I can do to change my teaching

the links to resources are really useful and I enjoyed arguing with the rest of the class

Closing the gap

Although the original CASAP materials were designed for staff based in Newcastle, the Information for Learning programme highlighted issues inherent in delivering the programme to staff from different countries and cultures. Not only do we need to consider that students have experienced a different learning culture, teaching staff are also accustomed to different teaching methods and this may reflect in the way they respond to information literacy concepts. Newcastle University is currently developing a presence overseas, with students and staff currently based in Singapore and Malaysia. A base parameter for all overseas initiatives is that staff and students should have parity of experience with their Newcastle-based peers, a clear challenge in terms of information literacy development and the Information for Learning resources. With these issues in mind, we were successful in receiving a University Innovation Fund award for 2011/12 to work specifically with colleagues based in Singapore.

The Newcastle University in Singapore (NUIS) Information Literacy Project

At the time of writing, this project is still under way. Snappily entitled 'Supporting and Embedding Information Literacy Development Opportunities into Teaching and Learning Practices between Overseas Partners' it comprises several practical strands. In its collaborative design and delivery it provides capacity-building opportunities for staff to embed information literacy concepts and an internationalized approach into their teaching practice. This will help both Newcastle-based staff, who are preparing teaching materials, and Singapore-based staff, who are delivering them, to better understand how information literacy can be developed within the curriculum. In providing a practical resource to help academic staff develop information-literate students, the project addresses the need to articulate the value of research-informed teaching to students by helping them to understand what research is and how it is done, as well as how to identify high-quality information. In this way, the project values diversity and embodies Newcastle University's vision to be 'globally ambitious and regionally rooted' (Newcastle University, 2009) exploiting the local knowledge and expertise of staff and students in Newcastle and Singapore to provide a common and constant learning experience.

An exciting and innovative aspect of the project is the way in which it makes connections at different levels across different boundaries. For example, it is hoped that addressing 'Information for Learning' issues with academic staff in both Newcastle and Singapore will highlight the alternative pedagogies which may exist between the different cultures and encourage consistency of delivery, giving staff support to embed the expectation of high-quality independent learning and research skills into their teaching.

Much of the content we are using for the NUIS project already exists, either in the Information for Learning programme or in the form of teaching resources developed for students. The challenge is how to repurpose the information to make it accessible to staff (and students) in both locations and more specifically to investigate whether the more discursive elements of the Information for Learning programme can be translated into an online environment. For the NUIS project two Blackboard online communities have been developed.

The NUIS Information for Learning Community

This pilot online Blackboard community is designed to be used initially by academic staff working in Singapore. The Singaporean staff include teachers who have worked in Newcastle University, those who have worked in other universities and staff who have worked predominantly in South East Asia. Concerns have been raised by the NUIS Dean that staff have very differing approaches to some information literacy concepts; areas relating to reflective writing, critical thinking, copyright, plagiarism and expectation of their students' ability to read around the subject have been specifically highlighted.

The Community aims to be a flexible workspace, into which staff can dip in and out and in which they can engage in discussion and debate with their peers. In its present iteration it is not linked to any guided learning programme and does not have to be worked through linearly, though this is recommended.

A parallel initiative at Newcastle, the UNITE project on e-learning and internationalization, enabled us to elicit feedback and make adjustments to the NUIS Communities before they went 'live'. Members of the UNITE network are people from across the university who have completed successful projects, are working in internationalization and/or e-learning or are currently starting on projects, so a mix of experienced and less experienced teachers. Meetings are designed to help participants discuss pedagogical issues relating to internationalization and e-learning, so the opportunity to focus a meeting on the NUIS project was a useful chance to test whether the kinds of materials and deliverables we were working on would work in a multicultural environment. We were able to discuss, for example, ideas for cascading pedagogical concepts relating to information literacy to academic staff in different cultures and explore how the academic staff might respond to being asked to work through the kinds of materials we planned to adapt from the face-to-face to the online environment. Pedagogical approaches to using e-learning materials were also addressed, as well as technical ideas from staff who have been using reusable learning objects in their own situations.

The NUIS Community was introduced to staff in Singapore in March 2012 and, at the time of writing, is being tested. One of the main issues surfacing in the pilot is that of initial engagement of staff with the materials, as there is no compulsion for them to participate, hence little formal evaluation has taken place so far. However, informal verbal feedback from the introductory sessions, as well as from the UNITE workshop, indicates that interest is focused on the concepts and ideas expressed in the Information for Learning and Information Literacy modules, with debate focusing on how the SCONUL Seven Pillars of Information Literacy model relates to South-East Asian teaching and learning styles. One very successful element of the face-to-face programme is the discussion relating to whether or not participants have ever, in their whole academic career, knowingly or unknowingly plagiarized. As differences surface, it is easy to make the point that if teachers can't agree, how difficult must it be for students? Reinforcement of this kind is much less effective in a more sanitized, non-synchronous, online discussion, even with the benefit of anonymity.

The NUIS Community introduces participants to ANCIL, inviting them to reflect on how they might use some of the suggested activities. I am hopeful that this very practical tool will facilitate the adoption of information literacy elements into the NUIS curricula.

The NUIS Research Skills for Students Community

The Information for Learning Community is partnered by a second community, NUIS Research Skills for Students. Figure 3.2 shows the look of the NUIS interface on the university website.

Although the community can be used as a standalone skills module by students, this is not its main purpose: our intention is for teaching staff to be able to copy elements from it into their own Blackboard modules and tailor them to the discipline context. In this way, it is hoped that the Blackboard community will eventually replace the Information Literacy Toolkit as a source of information literacy elements which can be easily integrated into the curriculum.

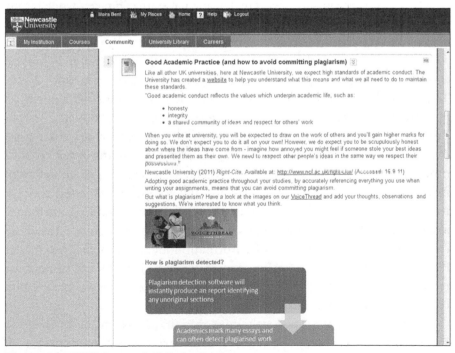

Figure 3.2 *NUIS Research Skills for Students*

Observation of the use of the community by students to date indicates a focus on evaluating and referencing information. Academic staff were asked to critically evaluate the content and suggest gaps and amendments and a clear steer has already been given to add more material on critical evaluation, in terms of both reading information and self-criticism of their own writing. A need for more detailed information on writing essays, reports and projects has also been identified, demonstrating that some staff view these academic literacies as part of becoming more information literate. Informal staff feedback from the pilot as well as the UNITE workshop indicates there is value in making the student resources more widely available to staff within the virtual learning environment (VLE).

Conclusions

Much of the work described above reflects my belief that information literacy needs to be perceived by teaching staff alongside their understanding of academic literacies. With this end in mind, activities, resources and projects are always designed in such a way that academic staff can take ownership of the manner in which their students develop their information literacy attributes.

My thinking has also been influenced by the work of Meyer and Land on threshold concepts and troublesome knowledge (Meyer and Land, 2003). They describe a threshold concept as representing a transformed way of understanding, interpreting or viewing something, without which a learner cannot progress. Crossing the threshold can be sudden, or may take place over a time period and can involve uncomfortable, counter-intuitive or in other words 'troublesome' knowledge. Making the shift in perception from information literacy being a purely skills- and competencies-based concept to one in which it is understood as a more complex blend of attributes, approaches and understanding fits well with the idea of recognizing threshold concepts in the development of information-literate people. One of my hopes for the Information for Learning programme is that it will bring some teaching staff to their own threshold in terms of appreciating the interrelation of information literacy and academic literacy.

Taking a pragmatic approach, however, it is already clear that the Information for Learning module will only have the desired impact if all the academic staff in the community engage with the materials. It has been suggested that the most effective approach may be to link the online materials to a face-to-face workshop, perhaps facilitated by those local teaching staff who have already experienced the CASAP programme and are information literacy 'champions'. As an alternative, we will also be working with the director of the CASAP programme to embed the Information for Learning materials into a new, online CASAP programme for wider dissemination.

Bibliography

Bent, M. and Brettell, S. (2006) What's Wrong With A Good Idea? An information literacy toolkit in practice, *ALISS Quarterly*, **2** (1).

Bent, M. and Stockdale, E. (2009) Integrating Information Literacy as a Habit of Learning: assessing the impact of a golden thread of IL in the curriculum, *Journal of Information Literacy*, **3** (1), 43–50.

Claxton, G. and Carr, M. A. (2004) A Framework for Teaching Learning: the dynamics of disposition, *Early Years*, **24**, 87–97.

Gourlay, L. (2009) Threshold Practices: becoming a student through academic literacies, *London Review of Education*, **7** (2), 181–92.

Lea, M. R. (2004) Academic Literacies: a pedagogy for course design, *Studies in Higher Education*, **29** (6), 739–56.

Lea, M. R. and Street, B. (1998) Student Writing in Higher Education: an academic literacies approach, *Studies in Higher Education*, **23** (2), 157–72.

Meyer, E. and Land, R. (2003) *Threshold Concepts and Troublesome Knowledge: linkages to ways of thinking and practising within the disciplines*, School of Education, University of Edinburgh, www.etl.tla.ed.ac.uk//docs/ETLreport4.pdf.

Newcastle University (2009) *Vision 2021: a world-class civic university*, www.ncl.ac.uk/documents/vision2021.pdf.

Perkins, D., Jay, E. and Tishman, S. (1993) Beyond Abilities: a dispositional theory of thinking, *The Merrill-Palmer Quarterly*, **39** (1), 1–21.

SCONUL Information Skills Task Force (1999) *Information Skills in Higher Education: a SCONUL position paper prepared by the SCONUL Advisory Committee on Information Literacy*, www.sconul.ac.uk/groups/information_literacy/papers/seven_pillars.html.

SCONUL Working Group on Information Literacy (2011) *The SCONUL Seven Pillars of Information Literacy: core model for higher education*, www.sconul.ac.uk/groups/information_literacy/seven_pillars.html.

Town, J. S. (2003) Information Literacy: definition, measurement, impact. In Martin, A. and Rader, H. (eds), *Information and IT Literacy: enabling learning in the 21st century*, Facet Publishing.

Wingate, U. (2006) Doing Away With 'Study Skills', *Teaching in Higher Education*, **11** (4), 457–69.

Strand Four

Mapping and evaluating the information landscape

Clare McCluskey

Strand Four focuses on developing students' awareness of the range of academic information formats available, together with their characteristics and their relative benefits. These include traditional formats such as monographs, textbooks and peer-reviewed journal articles, but in the digital age also embrace researcher blogs, open access journals and preprint repositories as well as open web pages.

A significant element in this strand is equipping students with the ability not only to recognize the variety of formats available and where and how to find them, but also to evaluate their appropriateness in the context of a specific task – e.g. an essay, a presentation, a dissertation. As in other strands, the focus is on enabling students to go beyond directed learning and achieve independent competence, mapping out the landscape of their subject for themselves and understanding the changing features of the information types within it.

We met Clare at the first of a series of workshops we delivered on ANCIL in 2011 and 2012, and were immediately struck by her work. Not only is she a prolific and articulate advocate of a broad, holistic view of information literacy, but her research into partnerships and communities of practice in higher education aligns very closely with ANCIL's interprofessional vision. Here she describes how this approach has enhanced students' understanding of the information landscape in education.

Institutional context

York St John University is a higher education institution with approximately 6000 students and 600 staff. Students study in one of four faculties/schools: the Faculty of Education and Theology, Faculty of Arts, Faculty of Health and Life Sciences or the York St John Business School. This case study takes place in the Faculty of Education and Theology, which is the largest in the university in terms of student numbers.

The library service is part of a converged team with ICT, referred to as Information Learning Services, and sits in the resources stream, along with facilities. Four academic support librarians work to bridge the gap to the faculties, which sit in the academic stream, one per faculty.

The approach outlined here is aligned with Initial Teacher Education courses, specifically the undergraduate BA(Hons) in Primary Education. Information literacy provision over the whole programme had been ad hoc and inconsistent, often relying on the opportunity to promote a new key resource, such as an e-book or new database, and tutors had reported students not retaining or applying the information skill techniques taught as part of this by the point they reached their third and final year. National Student Survey (NSS) scores in this area were showing a lack of engagement, with responses to the issue of library resources low, despite significant investment in new stock.

The academic support librarian wanted to increase collaboration with faculty to ensure better library input into the programme, improving the student experience of research and resource use. The academic support librarian had evidence of a lack of information skills in final-year primary education students from keeping a reflective diary of the queries she was answering. For example, a group of final-year students had requested help from the library in 'finding e-journals on literacy'. They showed no understanding of why they needed to find journals, electronic or print, what they were or whether they were appropriate for their information need. In further discussion, little knowledge of different types of information such as legislation, policy documents and reviews, conference papers, case studies, etc. was evident, nor did students know where to locate them (despite being directed to use them in assignments). During tutorials with the academic support librarian the students picked up these concepts quickly and stated a wish that they had had more input and direction in lectures throughout the course.

Gaps in information literacy provision were identified in discussions between the academic support librarian and module tutors. These discussions were recorded as unstructured interviews for a research project on information literacy promotion and the role of the academic librarian in the faculty (McCluskey, 2011). Examples of these gaps included the ability to identify and access key research to contextualize situations encountered in the classroom while on placement, and an awareness of the different ways of discovering and using policy information. It was also identified that an appreciation of other professionals and fellow students as part of a knowledge-sharing network should be encouraged.

How the module was developed

The first step had been discussions with academics regarding one another's roles and values, as outlined previously. This led to commitment to work together on areas where there were shared concerns – i.e. empowering students to become independent learners. 'I see our students as researchers. I see myself as a researcher, but there's that other in teaching-led institutions, that other bit where you are going out there and pulling it into your knowledge and moving it so they can be empowered' (Tutor B, 2010).

One particular opportunity for collaboration that resulted from these interviews was the involvement of the academic support librarian to be involved with research into the efficacy of one professional studies core module at level 3 of the course. This module was rooted in inquiry-based learning, encouraging the students to be independent learners. The module team and the research in question were concerned with putting the scaffolding in place to support this.

The first step was addressing the concerns of staff who requested further input on the concept of information literacy, so the academic support librarian designed a staff development opportunity with a focus on a discussion of the SCONUL Seven Pillars of Information Literacy (SCONUL, 1999) and how its concepts could be applied to the Primary Education programme. These sessions were run for groups and for individuals connected to the subject area of Primary Education, according to the preferences of different faculty members, so gave plenty of opportunity for attendance. They were kept to a one-hour duration, keeping in mind the time pressures felt by academics in the faculty, but with options for follow ups via phone, e-mail or in person if requested.

Collaboration

The information literacy input into the module was designed in collaboration with the module team and it was decided that the academic support librarian and faculty members would teach together in lectures. Collaboration was vital in this process, both between library and faculty and also between staff and students.

Primary Education courses have time pressures due to the need to fit in all necessary content for teacher training. The amount of time spent on placement is also an influence on how much time can be spent on teaching. As a professional studies core module, the one in question is compulsory for all students. This means 140 per year group, so it is difficult to arrange workshop groups, but it does mean that all of the students are reached. Discussions with the module leader established that several bite-sized sessions would both fit in with the timetable and help with reflective thinking throughout the module, offering appropriate input at an appropriate time. The academic support librarian then made herself available for follow-up tutorials in the following weeks. The module team wanted to foster the idea that students are responsible for their own learning, so arranging these follow-up tutorials was up to the students themselves. Motivation to do so was provided by a focus from the module team on student-led workshops and the assignments requiring reflection on literature in an area of their choice, linked to an issue encountered on placement.

Module content

The first step was to make explicit to the students the link between the input the library was giving and the module's key targets. The module has two key learning outcomes which link to information literacy:

* Analyse and critically evaluate on own emerging identity as a professional and engage in analytical dialogue regarding . . . teaching and learning.
* Critically discuss educational theory and concepts, drawn from academic study and school experience, and apply to . . . thinking about professional issues.

Information literacy input is also key to the first assignment:

- Give an individual presentation on a chosen feature of policies and procedures drawn from . . . current school setting and underpinned by reference to appropriate literature and legislation. This must demonstrate knowledge of Hodge's attributes of the student as a scholar and be supported by list of references (marked as part of assignment).

The concept of the 'student as scholar' outlined by Hodge et al. (2008) includes the following attributes:

Active Critical Thinking:
- Accepts responsibility for learning (active v. passive)
- Uses answers as an opportunity to ask more questions; is not constrained by the specific requirements of a course or project
- Understands multiple perspectives
- Has the ability to self critique

Research Skills:
- Lays out appropriate methodologies for scholarship generating or using original material
- Understands how to work collaboratively, even in a geographically dispersed team
- Integrates learning both within and across disciplines

Self-Authorship:
- Is internally motivated, not needing external pressures (like grades) to initiate work
- Believes he/she is capable of authoring new knowledge
- Judges new information based on personal values and belief system, rather than relying on external authorities
- Sees oneself as a member of a larger community of scholars and looks to peers in order to share viewpoints and contribute to the quality of critical dialogue

Hodge et al. (2008), 5–6

The module also includes student-led seminars where groups of students are responsible for identifying themes and literature on key topics.

The SCONUL Seven Pillars had been introduced to the module leader

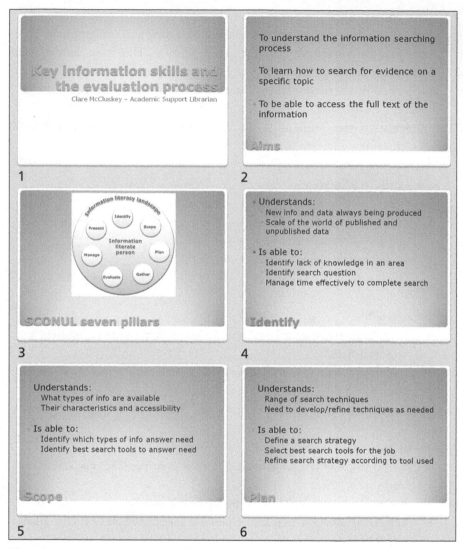

Figure 4.1a *Session 1 content, showing mapping to SCONUL Seven Pillars*

and she was keen to use this as a basis for the library input. The pillar diagram was posted in the module handbook before any input and the students were asked to refer to it and to Hodge's outline of the student as scholar, making links from both to the parts of the module outlined above.

Small, bite-sized inputs were designed by the academic support librarian to occupy the first ten minutes of module lectures, approximately once every

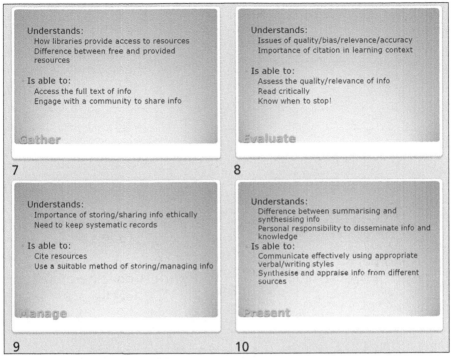

Understands:
How libraries provide access to resources
Difference between free and provided resources

Is able to:
Access the full text of info
Engage with a community to share info

Gather

7

Understands:
Issues of quality/bias/relevance/accuracy
Importance of citation in learning context

Is able to:
Assess the quality/relevance of info
Read critically
Know when to stop!

Evaluate

8

Understands:
Importance of storing/sharing info ethically
Need to keep systematic records

Is able to:
Cite resources
Use a suitable method of storing/managing info

Manage

9

Understands:
Difference between summarising and synthesising info
Personal responsibility to disseminate info and knowledge

Is able to:
Communicate effectively using appropriate verbal/writing styles
Synthesise and appraise info from different sources

Present

10

Figure 4.1b *Session 1 content, showing mapping to SCONUL Seven Pillars*

two weeks. These, too, were mapped against the Seven Pillars, so that the students could refer back to the theoretical model. The content of these bite-sized sessions was as follows:

Session 1

An introduction to the Seven Pillars, explanation of what they mean and how they fit with the programme. This was part of the first lecture of the module and therefore introduced together with all other context and expectations (see Figures 4.1a and 4.1b).

Session 2

Concentrates on the different types of information available and where to find them: for example, finding overviews of theories in textbooks, as opposed to finding critiques or research based upon them in journal articles.

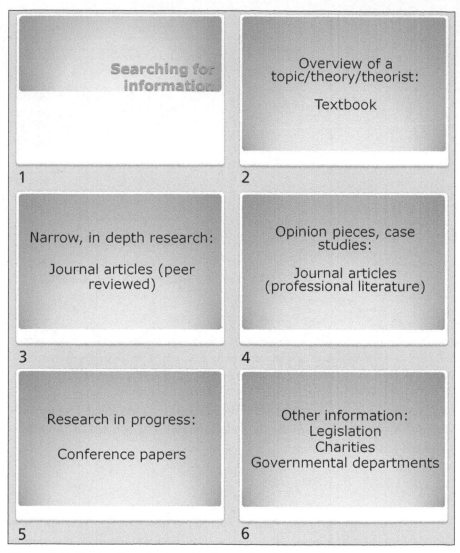

Figure 4.2 *Session 2 content: evaluating various information types*

The students have often used these different information formats but have never really thought about why, so now, when prompted, they can describe and reflect on why they are used in different circumstances (see Figure 4.2).

Mention is made of other types of information, such as conference papers for works in progress and case studies for more practical examples – these are generally new types of resource to the students.

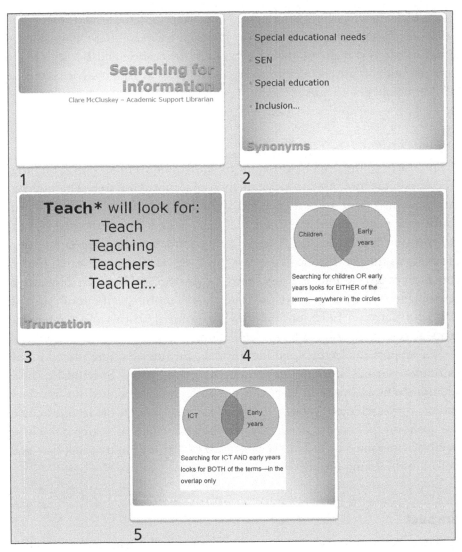

Figure 4.3 *Session 3 content: advanced keyword searching*

Session 3

The focus is on ensuring a good range of keywords are used in searching (see Figure 4.3). This programme does not require evidence of systematic searches in assessments, so there is no mention of plotting them on grids. Instead, reflection upon synonyms for popular search terms is encouraged, so that appropriate information is less likely to be missed. An example is given of a student who was interested in education in the armed forces, but who only thought about searching for the term 'military' after this session. A brief mention is made of the advantages of truncation and Boolean logic, and the students are encouraged to use the tutorials to ask for advice on these if they would like to pursue them.

Session 4 – final session of the term

This returns to the main types of information outlined in Session 2, but now focuses on the tools used to locate them in educational research. The students are now into their assessments and should be able to see what types of information are needed and where they can be used. This is the first session to mention individual search tools, so students are encouraged to begin searches as they have done in the past (by using our federated search tool in the main catalogue and, of course, the Google search!) However, this session encourages students to move on from this to more specific tools such as British Education Index or SocIndex[1] for journal articles and conference papers, and legislation.gov.uk for legislation.

To support the lectures and the tutorials, further aids were placed in the module's virtual learning environment (VLE) area. Specifically, help demonstrations (made in Captivate software) were designed on the finer points of searching in specific databases, so that time in the lectures could be spent on the more general, transferrable, principles of searching.[2] These were accompanied by links to key resource lists in the library catalogue[3] and a forum for asking further advice.

Impact

The first year this model ran, the academic support librarian received requests for seven follow-ups, seeing 16 students. During the second year this increased to eight follow-ups which covered 30 students, as they came in groups. Not much more of the librarian's time is needed, but more students are benefiting. Peer-to-peer help is also encouraged, as the students mention taking the advice back to those who could not make sessions. It is hoped this response rate will increase further the next time the module runs. This should be facilitated by librarians in the university who now have access to the institution-wide tutorial booker, which had not been the case during the first two years of input. This will make booking tutorials much easier, with one click replacing protracted e-mail approaches where available times are sent back and forth.

The NSS showed that satisfaction with the library in this particular programme increased by 3% in the lower primary cohort and 16% in the upper after the first iteration of the input. It will be mapped against the NSS again after the second and third iterations.

This approach has now been adapted for use in other programmes in the Education faculty, according to the needs of the cohort. For example, after consultation with the head of programme, it was decided that the full-time PGCE group (again with approximately 150 students) would receive longer workshops, in smaller groups. It was thought that more interaction should be required of them, so whereas the undergraduates are asked to reflect but not respond in the lectures, the PGCE groups are required to feed back to the academic support librarian and the group.

As this cohort consists of postgraduates, the main focus of sessions is on reflecting upon the tools they have used in their previous studies and their opinions of how useful they had been. Online polling tools such as Poll Everywhere have proved invaluable for collating these during the workshops – the academic support librarian could plot the students' responses to questions such as 'Which search tool did you find most useful in your previous studies?' on an iPad and choose when to display them to the group.

The sessions for the PGCE cohort proved invaluable in moving the students' thinking away from specific proprietorial resources. For example, when asked about the type of search tools they had used previously, many responded with answers such as 'JSTOR' or 'MetaLib' (tools to which York St John University library does not subscribe). By taking these responses and asking the students to reflect upon what they found in the tools and why they were useful, the cohort could begin to explore the types of evidence they needed and think about appropriate tools available to find them. This not only encouraged wider reflective thinking about information searching, but also allowed the academic support librarian to manage expectations through discussions about the ways that different universities subscribe to various resources.

Pedagogic principles

My main influence in taking the approach outlined in this chapter was the idea of communities of practice as proposed by Wenger (1998; 2006). He asserts that learning is a fundamentally social phenomenon and that mutual engagement is key to this:

> Practice does not exist in the abstract. It exists because people are engaged in actions whose meanings they negotiate with one another . . . Membership in a community of practice is therefore a matter of mutual engagement.
>
> Wenger (1998, 73)

> Communities of practice are groups of people who share a concern or passion for something they do and learn how to do it better as they interact regularly.
>
> Wenger (2006, 1)

Wenger (2006, 1–2) asserts that there are three crucial characteristics in a community of practice:

1   The domain – a shared domain of interest and a commitment to this.
2   The community – members partake in joint activities and discussions.
3   The practice – members develop a shared repertoire of resources.

Reflecting upon this, it struck me that what was lacking was effective communication between the library and the faculty, and a joint approach to information skills, with each group taking into account the aims and values of the other. Previous attempts to embed information literacy in the curriculum had tended to be top-down, with little engagement with those formulating and teaching programmes and modules. Communities of practice emerge from members having joint aims and values and I could not believe that the librarians did not share at least some of these with faculty members, in relation to the student experience.

In this instance, the domain is a commitment to ensuring that students have the scaffolding they need to be effective professionals, including research and information skills. The community is the module or programme team, which is focused upon sharing expertise in its design. The practice is the delivery of the module or programme content. This was what informed my decision to use conversation with faculty members about learning and teaching as a basis for taking information literacy input forward.

Notes

1   www.bei.ac.uk; www.ebscohost.com/public/socindex.
2   Examples of demonstrations can be seen at
    http://library.yorksj.ac.uk/tutorials/BEI/ and
    http://library.yorksj.ac.uk/tutorials/findingarticles/findingarticles.htm.
3   e.g. http://yorksj.worldcat.org/profiles/YSJITE/lists/1888957.

Bibliography

Hodge, D., Haynes, C., Le Pore, P., Pasquesi, K. and Hirsh, M. (2008) From Inquiry to Discovery: developing the student as scholar in a networked world. In *Learning through Enquiry Alliance (LTEA) Conference, 25–27 June, University of Sheffield*, http://cilass-resources.group.shef.ac.uk/ltea2008/Hodge_CETL_2008_keynote.pdf.

McCluskey, C. (2011) Creating Information Literacy Partnerships in Higher Education, *Library and Information Research*, **35** (111), 59–72.

SCONUL Information Skills Taskforce (1999) *Seven Pillars of Information Literacy*, SCONUL, www.sconul.ac.uk/groups/information_literacy/seven_pillars.html.

Tutor B (2010) What is My Understanding of the Role of an Academic Support Librarian? [Interview], York St John University with C. McCluskey, 20 April 2010.

Wenger, E. (1998) *Communities of Practice: learning meaning and identity*, Cambridge University Press.

Wenger, E. (2006) Communities of Practice: a brief introduction, http://wenger-trayner.com/Intro-to-CoPs.

Strand Five

Resource discovery in your discipline

Isla Kuhn

Where Strand Four deals with the various publication formats in which scholarly information is made available, Strand Five focuses on the gateways, platforms and collection-level resources which endeavour to aggregate these formats. Libraries are key players in making these resources available, including not only library and archival catalogues but also abstract and indexing databases, subject-specific gateways, e-journal collections and datasets. In addition, library websites also act as informal aggregators, linking to other academic resources.

Therefore, in addition to being aware of the different types of information available in the academic landscape, students need to learn to locate, use and, above all, evaluate the containers or gateways through which they access them. Because of their size, it is not always evident that these key 'finding aids' themselves have limitations of scope, coverage or chronology, and that critical evaluation must be applied not only to individual scholarly works, but also to whole resources.

Isla has helped pioneer several teaching initiatives in the University of Cambridge library community, including the TeachMeet format and events, a '23 Things' course tailored for medical library staff, and mutual peer observation of teaching. She was the natural choice for Strand Five, as she teaches students where to look for and how to evaluate complex specialist information, not in a programmatic way but using a discursive and reflective approach that develops a deep understanding of the advantages and limitations of the resources and databases themselves as information tools. Isla was also an Arcadia Fellow in 2011, organizing a high-profile symposium and 'hackday' on 'The Internet-Informed Patient' (www.iip-symposium.info/).

Institutional context

As Reader Services Librarian in the University of Cambridge Medical Library, my role is all about supporting readers in their research, education or clinical care. Readers come from a range of backgrounds and are at various stages in their academic and professional careers. Clinical students naturally form a major group. These students have completed up to three years of pre-clinical studies either in Cambridge or at other universities, but this does not necessarily help them gain awareness of the sources of clinical – as opposed to academic – information that will be valuable for them. Students arriving from other universities face challenges in terms of adapting to a new information environment and, in particular, discovering a different range of subscription resources.

Similarly, many postgraduates may have come from a different university and/or a different country, so may not be familiar with the resources that University of Cambridge has to offer (or they may need to learn to navigate their way through a different presentation of the resources). These postgraduates are also dealing with a significant leap in expectation of skills and scale of the task they have taken on.

Practising clinicians use the library to support clinical care. In addition, they are frequently also involved in postgraduate study, research or ongoing professional development. Again, they may have come from another NHS trust and may not be familiar with the way resources and databases are organized in Cambridge. Finally, researchers at every stage in their career make use of the Medical Library's facilities and online resources, while students from other universities use the Medical Library when they are on placement in the hospital. As well as being aware of what resources each group of library users are entitled to use, it is important to consider what is relevant to the task they have ahead of them, so that the appropriate resources can be highlighted in a timely fashion.

Two different types of teaching scenario will be used in this chapter to illustrate Strand Five. The first is a half-day course taught by me, called Systematic Literature Reviews – A 'How To' Guide; the second is an innovative peer teaching initiative which trains student champions for the NHS Evidence database.

Literature searching in the clinical medicine field

Postgraduates who find themselves with the task of carrying out a systematic literature review of their topic often find that the skills they developed at undergraduate level are not quite up to the job ahead. These learners have often managed to get through their undergraduate studies without ever having to do much independent research; even when they have completed an undergraduate dissertation this is unlikely to have involved a literature search of the rigour that is necessary at postgraduate level in the clinical field. Within health and medical research, systematic reviews of the existing literature or 'evidence' are hugely valuable. They are often seen as 'quick wins' when early-career researchers are considering a first publication. However, this perception is hugely out of synch with the realities of the work that is involved in this type of publication. First-year PhD students are required to produce a report which includes a literature review on their area of research. Missing relevant papers at this stage could jeopardize subsequent work through duplication of effort, or – more dangerously – inaccurate baseline assumptions.

Working across disciplines is becoming increasingly common in postgraduate research. Leaving the comfort zone of the undergraduate discipline highlights inadequacies in students' knowledge of sources of information, and often leads them to question their awareness of information resources in their own field. The sheer scale of the work ahead of them in terms of information management and maintaining an awareness of relevant resources and databases will also be new and daunting. Students very likely managed to cope with handwriting the references for their undergraduate dissertation. This will not be realistic for their postgraduate work – three years' worth of references and accumulated full text papers need a strategy to manage them.

These are some of the reasons I have created the half-day session Systematic Literature Reviews – a 'How To' Guide. This workshop is aimed at science postgraduates in general, and those working in life sciences and medicine specifically. It is delivered to groups of up to ten, which allows for small-group work, and is designed to create a supportive environment for both individual questions and large group discussion. What the 'How To' course aims to do is to encourage the attendees to question and develop their approach when faced with the task of undertaking a systematic literature review, considering where might be appropriate for them to search, what different types of information might be necessary to include, and how to manage the output.

Systematic Literature Reviews – a 'How To' Guide

The course aims to address:

- how to clarify the question (or perhaps questions) on which you need to find literature
- how to select the databases and other resources you will need to search
- how to devise the most comprehensive literature search strategy, so you know you have not missed any relevant studies
- how to keep up to date with new information appearing between the initial search and write-up
- issues around documentation of process and results
- management of references (using software such as EndNote), and getting hold of the full-text article.

The session starts with introductions. Students are invited to introduce themselves and give a brief idea of their hopes and expectations of the course. These are noted on a flipchart and referred to throughout the course. It helps to reassure the students that they are all in the same situation and they are not the only one who is feeling unsure or ill-prepared for the task ahead. Students are also asked what experience they have of carrying out literature searching. Acknowledging the expertise in the room is important, not least because the students can learn as much from each other's experience as from the trainer. The students are encouraged to ask questions throughout the course.

The students will very likely come from a variety of academic disciplines. This is important to acknowledge early on in the session, but equally it is important to highlight the fact that the principles, tools and methods of searching for literature are generic, and the students will be using their own research question in the session as much as possible. This will influence their choice of resource, so it is crucial that they develop an understanding of the scope, content and limitations of appropriate databases.

The first exercise is to try to decipher a search strategy that was created to find evidence for a high-quality systematic review (see Figure 5.1). This is partly a scare tactic highlighting the difference between the students' current

1 clinical trial.pt.	24 or/13-23	46 exp Bed Rest/
2 randomized.ab,ti.	25 exp Spine/	47 bed rest.mp.
3 placebo.ab,ti.	26 discitis.ab,ti.	48 or/39-47
4 dt.fs.	27 exp Spinal Diseases/	49 24 or 38
5 randomly.ab,ti.	28 (disc adj degeneration).ab,ti.	50 12 and 49
6 trial.ab,ti.	29 (disc adj prolapse).ab,ti.	51 48 and 50
7 groups.ab,ti.	30 (disc adj herniation).ab,ti.	
8 or/1-7	31 spinal fusion.sh.	
9 Animals/	32 spinal neoplasms.sh.	
10 Humans/	33 (facet adj joints).ab,ti.	
11 9 not (9 and 10)	34 intervertebral disk.sh.	
12 8 not 11	35 postlaminectomy.ab,ti.	
13 dorsalgia.ab,ti.	36 arachnoiditis.ab,ti.	
14 exp Back Pain/	37 (failed adj back).ab,ti.	
15 exp Low Back Pain/	38 or/25-37	
16 backache.ab,ti.	39 exp activities of daily living/	
17 (lumbar adj pain).ab,ti.	40 activities of daily living.tw.	
18 coccyx.ab,ti.	41 day to day activ$.ti,ab.	
19 coccydynia.ab,ti.	42 daily activit$.ti,ab.	
20 exp Sciatica/	43 ordinary activit$.ti,ab.	
21 sciatica.ab,ti.	44 normal activit$.ti,ab.	
22 spondylosis.ab,ti.	45 stay$ active.ti,ab.	
23 lumbago.ab,ti.		

Figure 5.1 *Example search strategy*

search techniques and the example. However, it also demonstrates the level of complexity that might be required for them to be sure that they are finding all the relevant literature. The most common concerns for these students is that they either want to find 'everything' on their topic, or they want to be sure that no one else has written about their topic. Either way, the search strategy has to be thorough. The students are asked to note down the research question that this strategy is finding the evidence to answer, and to put it on one side.

The session then moves on to consider the main building blocks of any search strategy – clarifying the question, using the PICO acronym (Patient, Intervention, Comparison, Outcome) as a method of identifying keywords and synonyms in the research question, applying Boolean operators and truncation.

After working through and demonstrating the principles with a generic example the students are then given a search grid, and time is allocated for them to work through their own research question. Individual support is offered as required, and this often helps to identify gaps in understanding of the principles. The students are then invited to swap their search grid with their neighbour. This allows them to discuss their own topic, and also to have a fresh set of eyes consider the way they're approaching the topic. Often mistakes in application of Boolean logic are picked up at this stage.

It is also valuable to have assumptions questioned. Many students will search, for example, for evidence of the value of physiotherapy interventions using variations of the word 'physiotherapy' as well as the specific exercise and the illness. However, in much physiotherapy research, the term 'physiotherapy' and its variations are absent. It is often assumed by the author that the fact that an exercise therapy is used as an intervention in patients with a particular illness makes it obvious that a physiotherapist has been involved – doesn't it? The student often needs to be encouraged to consider the assumptions they are making.

Resource selection and evaluation

Having got the basics of the search strategy worked out, there is an opportunity for 'play'. The database Web of Science (http://wok.mimas. ac.uk/) is usually used at this point, since it is multi-disciplinary, so there is generally something for everyone. Students log on and test out their new strategy. They are able to compare the results of this style of searching with their existing awareness of the literature (which often brings groans of 'oh dear, there's so much more to read!' as well as satisfied noises that indicate that they recognize some of the hits).

At this point I introduce discussion on the scope of different databases and why the students might not be finding all the articles that they're aware of. Since all the students have already done a lot of reading around the topic, the fact that their search does not pull up everything they are familiar with is one of the first comments that is made. I suggest there are two possible reasons for this: that their search is not quite sensitive enough yet (i.e., they have not used all the keywords they will need to find all the relevant articles), or that the database they are currently using does not index all the relevant journals. Although of course no single database will contain every journal that might be relevant, some have such a strong subject focus that students may feel they are sufficient for certain pieces of work. Students are sometimes surprised to discover that this is not the case, since their main point of reference, Google, does cover 'everything' (they believe).

The fact that some of the more relevant databases require a login is often one of the biggest obstacles to their use. One of the major health and medicine resources, Medline, is freely available via PubMed. Other relevant resources such as Embase, PsycINFO and CINAHL are all behind an institutional login, and consequently awareness of these tools is lower.[1]

Generally the students attending this course all have one bibliographic database in common (apart from Google Scholar, that is) – PubMed. This allows me to assess the level of complexity of the students' current search strategies, and offers an opportunity to introduce MeSH – the system of medical subject headings applied in PubMed. Often students have heard of it, even if they are not using it actively. The benefits and impact that use of subject headings can have on a search strategy is demonstrated with a generic search, and again the students have an opportunity to experiment. MeSH can open students' eyes to the variety of language around a subject, which will improve their searching in other databases. Having already carried out a search in Web of Science earlier in the session the students now have an opportunity to test their newly crafted search strategy in PubMed, taking advantage of the subject headings. This allows for some cross-database comparison, but I also direct students to guides to using a range of databases such as the 'Big Four' databases in life sciences – PubMed, Embase, Web of Science and Scopus (www.scopus.com).

Sometimes a lack of awareness of other relevant databases results from the move into cross-disciplinary research, and students struggle to identify the 'PubMed equivalent' in the new discipline. As well as giving some statistics on the number of journal titles covered by different databases, and the amount of overlap of coverage, I show the students a page on the library website that organizes the databases by subject, which they can explore. Knowing where to look for a list of possible relevant databases in a subject area is important (usually available on library websites), and knowing where they can turn to for help when considering the needs of their particular research question (the librarian!) is vital.

Following this, students are invited to consider the different sorts of information they might need to include in their work. While journal literature might form the core of their reading, it is important they at least consider (even if they later discount) other forms of information: books, currently ongoing research, statistics or data sets, grey literature. These all have their different sources and methods necessary for searching for them. For example, the registers of current trials only allow for very limited keyword searching; the library catalogue is great for books, but they might also want to consider a wider catalogue such as COPAC (http://copac.ac.uk) to search beyond Cambridge library holdings. Students are encouraged to identify key organizations, royal colleges, research institutions, blogs etc., which are relevant to their work, and to explore these web pages or publications as further specialist sources of information.

This point in the workshop usually raises the question of searching in Google – what the difference is between using Google Scholar and databases such as PubMed. In my experience there is usually at least one student who is aware of the issues of personalization of Google searches, so they are encouraged to share their understanding with the group. There is also an opportunity to raise awareness of more sophisticated search techniques in Google – using inverted commas for a phrase search, or running site-specific or filetype-specific searches.

The nature of a systematic literature review is that the methodology must be reproducible and transparent, just in the same way that a lab experiment that turns wood into gold will only be of value if the method is replicable. I raise questions with the students about how they might prioritize the articles they might want to read – perhaps on the basis of age of literature, type of article, study design or language of article. Pros and cons of each method are discussed, and again issues of bias are discussed. The students now experiment with limiting their own search strategy. The discussion is taken a stage further and inclusion and exclusion criteria are introduced, together with the concept that for a sound methodology the reasons why articles are excluded from further reading or analysis must be explicit. The students are encouraged to keep notes and logs of their work, to save their search strategies, so they can write up their methodology accurately, and not just give a hazy account from memory.

The discussion and exercises assist students to gain familiarity not just with how the databases work in functional terms, but also with their potential limitations. This should enable them to make an informed choice about where to search for literature and evidence, not just how.

Managing information and maintaining awareness of the field

The final stages of the Systematic Literature Review – a 'How to' Guide workshop are taken up with considering how to manage the references that are generated by searches. This covers issues of critical appraisal of the literature, use of reference management software and data extraction. Again, student experience is elicited and shared as much as possible: why do they use one reference management tool rather than another? Have they considered the features that will be most important to them? Which would they recommend? Answers are noted on a flipchart for reference and discussion.

The question of data extraction relates to 'future-proofing' the information that students find. Here I ask the question: if they came back in six weeks' time would they know why they had kept a particular article? It also raises issues of analysis and comparison of the data: how will they quickly compare the results of one study with another? What are the key measures they need to identify? The more thought that can go into this process in advance, the less time-consuming re-reading will be necessary.

The undergraduate dissertation experience does not often require much in the way of keeping abreast of current developments. Postgraduate work, however, does. Again, student experience and existing methods of current awareness are drawn out through discussion. Choices are offered, since this can often help general efficiency – suggesting RSS feeds rather than e-mail alerts can help students manage their time better, and at the very least it sheds light on what that odd orange square was doing on all the web pages the students use. The use of citation tracking is often a new concept to the students. The prospect of being alerted any time their own work is cited is generally enough to encourage them to explore further, while they also recognize the value of discovering competing researchers by being alerted when citing the same key work.

For this course the definition of 'resource' is very broad, ranging from the search techniques of Boolean logic and subject headings to the databases that are searched, and also including information management tools and current awareness tools. The discovery and adoption of a range of resources and tools is fundamental to a thorough and rigorous – indeed systematic – literature review, which in turn provides the foundation for future research and clinical practice. The 'Systematic Literature Reviews' course, while focusing on content from Strand Five, touches on many aspects of the ANCIL curriculum.

NHS Evidence student champions: a peer teaching initiative

NHS Evidence (www.evidence.nhs.uk) is a service created and maintained by NICE (National Institute of Health and Clinical Excellence) that enables access to authoritative clinical and non-clinical evidence and best practice through a web-based portal. Offering a 'Google-style' search interface, it is easy to use, approachable, and offers a manageable number of high-quality hits on clinical topics. For clinical students feeling overwhelmed at the amount of information available, and for busy clinicians who just want an answer quickly, it is a very valuable resource.

NHS Evidence is keen to train student champions as a means of encouraging use of the resource. A programme of 'train the trainers' courses has been rolled out across a number of universities offering medical, nursing and pharmacy courses, and the student champions then deliver training to their peers. The 'train the trainers' course is delivered over one day in London at the NICE offices, and a half day back at the host institution. Students gain a deeper understanding of NICE and of the scope and purpose of NHS Evidence. They are given guidance on teaching and an opportunity to explore the resource itself. Attending this course as a group develops a peer support and teaching framework. Three schools were involved in the initial pilot, a further five came on board later in 2011 (NICE, 2011), and eight students from University of Cambridge Clinical School participated in early 2012.

Champions each deliver two sessions to their peers, in pairs or groups if preferred, and write a short report reflecting on their experience. The training is evaluated so that impact can be measured. Students attending the peer-led session are surveyed in advance of the session to gauge baseline awareness of NHS Evidence and current searching strategies. They are also canvassed for 'real' research questions that can be used in the training. These questions are given to the champions so that they can tailor their teaching. There is a brief evaluation immediately after the session to measure how useful students thought the resource was and what they thought of the teaching they had received, and the champions receive a copy of the feedback relating to their own sessions. Three months after the training, the students are surveyed one more time to measure retention of knowledge.

Librarian support for the students in their teaching and learning is seen as a vital component to the success of these sessions. At the request of the champions, I supported them in their communication with the Clinical School, attended the training with them, and supported their organization and delivery of sessions to their peers (this included giving advice on room booking and how students would sign up for one of the champion-delivered sessions). The training was all hands-on, using the student learners' own research questions to demonstrate functionality. During the sessions themselves I was very much in the background, only taking an active part if there were technical issues or if the champions struggled to answer a more complex question. For example, in one session there were problems with the data projector which required a 'Heath Robinson' solution involving loading a PowerPoint presentation onto Google Docs and creating a short URL to share with the participants, who then toggled between it and NHS Evidence under the direction of the champions. The champions coped admirably! Students also asked questions about resources beyond the scope of NHS Evidence, including e-books and access to online journals. I was able to contribute when the champions were unsure.

This approach had a number of benefits. The student champions gained valuable teaching experience. The student learners, who were all in the first year of their clinical studies, benefited from having champions coming from all three year groups. The champions were able to raise awareness of how familiarity with NHS Evidence would help the students in future tasks and projects: the older champions were able to identify how they would have used NHS Evidence with a project 'if only they'd known', and the younger champions were able to pass this experience on during their sessions. By attending all the courses I was able to take the opportunity to remind students that support for research and learning was available from the library at any point after the training session. I was also able to get useful insight into what the students consider valuable in an information resource, and how I might present it in the future to best support their learning in this area.

Conclusion

My teaching sessions are never one-way, and the constructivist approach I use is fundamental to their success. There is always the opportunity for me to gain a better understanding of what students wish to achieve by attending, and thereby adapting the session to make it more relevant. Any situation which brings students together is an opportunity for them to learn from each other. This is especially true for the postgraduates who often work in relative isolation, particularly compared with their undergraduate experience. Advice that comes from a peer is just as valuable as that which comes from an expert, perhaps more so if the expert is knowledgeable about the resource that is being explored, but not the particular context in which it will be used (e.g. while I have studied to Masters level, I have not done a PhD).

Working in small groups and encouraging discussion and comment at every stage allows everyone to consider the comments and reactions of their peers as well as hearing from me. While I can list the difference between various reference management tools and teach the students how to use them all, hearing why a peer changed from using one to another will almost always be of more interest. Hearing that a peer found new, highly relevant articles when they searched in a second database (and which second database they used), rather than just relying on one source, will be more convincing that my telling the students why they really should search more than one database. Overall, hearing how peers are scoping the information landscape and selecting the best tools and resources is hugely valuable for students.

Notes

1   PubMed: www.ncbi.nlm.nih.gov/pubmed/; Embase: www.embase.com; PsycINFO: www.apa.org/psycinfo/; CINAHL: www.library.nhs.uk/help/resource/cinahl.

Bibliography

NICE (2011) *The NHS Evidence Student Champion Scheme: an introduction for university staff*, www.evidence.nhs.uk/documents/s-engagement-management-marketing-communications-public-relations-student-champions-scs-promotional-materials-nhs4571-student-champions-lores.pdf.

Strand Six

Managing information

Elizabeth Tilley

Strand Six includes a range of key functional skills such as time management and planning, effective information storage and retrieval, reference management and staying up to date. Without these skills students will struggle to manage and process academic information efficiently. While the practical element of these skills is taught widely, it is important to emphasize that there is a cognitive aspect inherent in each which links the daily practices of study and research directly to the learner's developing identity. It is therefore vital to give students the opportunity to reflect on how they will integrate these skills into their own practices and workflow, and to review their practices from time to time.

Many digital tools are available to support and simplify these aspects of information management, and trainers are free to select and teach the tools they feel are most appropriate for a particular cohort at a given time. We have not stipulated particular tools to teach, firstly since technology is moving at too fast a pace, and secondly in order to emphasize that understanding the underlying study and research needs is of greater importance than learning to use specific tools or programs to aid these processes.

As the Librarian at the Faculty of English at the University of Cambridge, Elizabeth has been teaching information literacy in a way that underpins many of the ANCIL principles. She was part of the expert consultation carried out as part of the ANCIL research and her thinking helped shape ideas about how the curriculum should be taught. Her approach to teaching students how to manage information, by using Zotero to engage them and provide the 'wow' factor, is a useful example of good practice in one of the key strands in any information literacy teaching.

Institutional context

The Faculty of English at the University of Cambridge is one of many faculties and departments which are organized loosely into schools; English is within the Arts and Humanities School. The majority of the faculties within this school have large, currently independently run, faculty libraries. Our priority at the English Faculty Library (EFL) in terms of collection development is with the undergraduate body, which comprises approximately 700 students. The largely taught MPhil programme at the faculty is active and increasingly an important aspect of provision, and as a result the library finds itself in the position of supporting this group as well. The total postgraduate body at any one time is about 200 students.

Undergraduates in the Faculty of English generally receive academic teaching in small, or singleton, supervisions or tutorials, within their college environment. An element of inconsistency in what is offered at this very local level means that students have a variable diet of information literacy teaching. As a result, a teaching programme devised by the Faculty Library for the undergraduates has been developed over the last three to four years. It focuses on addressing the needs of students at specific points in their undergraduate course, and has some elements that are fully embedded within the course structure of the faculty, with others based on an assumption that faculty and students will engage with the teaching on a voluntary basis. Progression throughout the programme is important.

Although much of our focus in teaching has been with undergraduates, specific opportunities in the area of information management have opened up with the postgraduates, too. Postgraduates are expected to develop their information literacy skills by making use of the courses on offer from various central bodies within the university. As discussed below, this does not always 'hit the spot' as far as students are concerned. It is primarily these needs and resulting workshops that have been developed for the postgraduate community that I will be considering in this chapter, although some further reference to our undergraduate teaching is included.

Working in an environment such as the University of Cambridge poses potential problems. On the one hand, there are sessions run centrally covering tools to manage information, but with a range of subjects to deal with they frequently remain too generic, and application to specific student issues and needs is problematic. Take-up of software or ideas following a session such as this is typically low. On the other hand, with each faculty having a library with specialist library staff and therefore with a unique opportunity of understanding the local context, it is possible to tailor sessions to specific needs. So, if I am running a session for graduates in the Faculty of English I can guarantee that it will not be replicated in its exact form elsewhere and what is delivered will be focused and relevant.

Student needs

To have an impact in what we do we must address needs, and this is a key part of the ANCIL approach to information literacy. The question is – what are the needs of English Literature students in the area of managing information? These are some of the key issues that I believe are relevant:

1   Students need to retrieve information effectively, recording all the relevant data about that information for future referencing; they also need to differentiate between the sources they save, understanding the elements of a citation.
2   They need some form of strategy in place for effective storage – 'effective' usually means a system which is easily searchable, organized and efficient and quick to back up, and fits within their research workflows. Importantly, students who spend most of their time with print materials may find that a technical solution to managing information incompatible with their work. It cannot be assumed that this is the best solution for all.
3   They need to save and manage time and effort, and will be looking for strategies or systems that remove some of the more machine-like formatting of references in general, specifically creating footnote and bibliography referencing, leaving more time for the reflective thinking that goes alongside deep reading of texts.

How to teach students to improve their information management skills varies, but it's useful to have a tool such as Zotero (www.zotero.org), a free and easy-to-use reference manager, to illustrate how managing information is a key to developing those skills and improving the capacity for learning. How this is incorporated into a session varies depending on the level of the student. However, this will be the focus of my case study.

Undergraduate teaching

In undergraduate dissertation classes information management is the core thread that weaves in and out of the session, where we start the group class off by thinking about what information they need to collect and how to store it, and work out what their current strategies for doing this are. This is followed by an interactive element considering which catalogues, databases and other relevant resources can be used to search for information. The students are encouraged to explore the resources, consider their search strategies and learn to make decisions about which results will be useful, so that there is a body of data that they collect during this stage of the session. This process also helps to highlight their need to manage this information.

We also spend time at this stage ensuring that students are clear about exactly what types of information they need to collect, and how they will use it in citing references within a dissertation or weekly essay context. Students vary in their referencing skills at this stage, so Zotero is used to illustrate not only the importance of selection criteria, and how to organize and analyse information, but also how it can assist with referencing. Essentially it makes sense to teach them a simple but effective system for saving and citing a reference alongside the activity of searching a database for useful information.

Postgraduate teaching

With a different audience – such as the postgraduate and academic community – we use Zotero, in its own right, as the rationale (and promotion) for the session. Two years ago it might have been EndNote; the tool itself is not important, it's merely there to provide the opportunity for students to reflect on their current practices and make appropriate changes.

There is a certain expectation that graduates need to learn about reference management tools to help them with their research, and we can use this expectation as a launchpad for the session that we devise. Potential attendees will almost certainly have some form of strategy for managing information in place, but, along with expecting to learn new skills, may well be looking for a more flexible, time-saving device that fits in with their research work flows.

Principles for teaching: pedagogy

Decisions about teaching activities for running a session with graduates are in turn dependent on pedagogical principles. Over time I have developed teaching programmes that are informed by my knowledge and understanding of the learning process. My background as a teacher, together with my own experience alongside understanding my own preferences for learning, have helped to form the basis of what I do. I have to revisit the rationale for what I do regularly to make sure that I am not too biased!

The primary focus for what I do is informed by the following principles:

1   Experiential learning: Kolb's (1984) theory in effect says that trying something out, reflecting on it, leads to learning through refinement. My main focus in redeveloping a small open study space in the library to make a multipurpose classroom was precisely to encourage this type of learning. The principle that says 'if you "do" something you are more likely to remember it' is key.

2   Related to this is my personal tendency to the activist and pragmatic learning styles as described by Honey and Mumford (2000). I am so strongly drawn to planning activities that are activist or pragmatist in nature that I have now incorporated a reflection in my planning grid that forces me to consider the theorist or reflector learning style alongside my own preferences.

3   Co-agency: this principle, described in the Learning Without Limits project at the University of Cambridge Faculty of Education (Hart et al., 2004), refers to constructing a teaching environment that is interactive and depends as much on what the attendees bring to the session as what the course leaders contribute. In developing a local tailored teaching session, this is really important and allowing the students time and space to bring their information management strategies to the table is important. Valuing what they do and demonstrating that we are learning from them builds trust and develops relationships.

    Underlying this is the 'principle of everybody', where the peer group is developed to create a community of learners who support and increase each other's learning capacity. We try to foster an integrated learning community with more collaborative tendencies and an appreciation of the benefits of learning from one another. The knock-on effect is that learning continues informally over the issue desk, through e-mail communications, ask-a-librarian queries and so on.

4   Ultimately a learning theory that informs teaching must be based on

conversations and interactions and an understanding of the needs in the faculty. This relational aspect of developing the learner is helpful. By definition, what suits one set of students or users will not necessarily suit another. For example, when I ran a recent session ran on using Zotero I included academics in the invitation; a feel for what academics perceive to be an ideal learning environment when alongside graduates is important.

These principles are broadly in line with those that underpin ANCIL. Collaborative learning based on real needs is a strong element proposed by ANCIL. One of the key information literacy attributes that is mentioned in the curriculum documents is that of transformation. In my view this can best be arrived at by developing training that rests on the collaborative pedagogic principles described above. Transforming student practice, I believe, is possibly longer lasting when peers are involved. In the postgraduate world there is a real need to break down barriers that exist between students based on assumptions of what they each know, and to encourage the sharing of best practice. A learning environment where best practice is shared and discussed and where advances in understanding are made collaboratively not only results in a student acquiring new skills, or changing their research habits, but also gives them the permission to say that they do not always know what the answer is, and to understand that others are in the same boat as them. We hope that they will take the collaborative approach out of the classroom and into their day-to-day lives.

The pedagogic principles above also reflect the active, inquiry-based learning that the ANCIL curriculum favours for information literacy development that in turn rests on the premise that an audit will have taken place to ascertain real needs.

Format and function of sessions

The development of an information literacy session at the Faculty of English often comes about following conversations between library staff and graduates and academics. Teaching sessions are often most successful, in both take-up and engagement, when the gap or need is one that the users have identified and, following discussions with them, we work together on putting a session together. Clearly this fits in with the key pedagogical rationale underlying the work we do, and with the ANCIL philosophy.

Timing is crucial, and local knowledge informs what we do. The ideal scenario for working with the postgraduates is an introductory workshop specifically targeted at the MPhil group covering the essentials of information management in the Michaelmas Term (October), and a follow-up interactive workshop in late January following their first piece of course work. This is the time when the penny begins to drop regarding their need to improve information literacy skills. However, constraints in the form of contributor availability – we were determined to have representation from both the academic and postgraduate body, as well as library staff this year – mean that in some respects I consider the format of the session to take precedence over the timing.

Once the key elements of the session are in place – content that is a response to local need, pedagogic principles applied, contributors and overall session format decided, and finally the timing – then the details of the session are mapped into a planning grid. The grid is especially useful for making sure that the class is really focused on the discussed needs of the users, but is set within the broader need to develop their overall research skills.

Planning

Planning teaching sessions where I am often in the role of 'facilitator' as much as 'teacher', I find that a prompt in the form of a grid – reminding us to think through all the issues, from learning outcomes right the way from the nuts and bolts of who does what and when, through to evaluation and assessment – is really helpful. If I teach on my own I have a tendency to forget to use this – generally at the cost of the students! So, the details of the session which forms the basis for this case study are set out in the grid that I used for the three presenters in the session. A form of the grid is now used for our undergraduate teaching where it is rare to have a session that does not have at least two 'trainers/teachers' in the session, and in fact often a 'peer' teacher taking part as well. The grid outline is in Figure 6.1, while Figure 6.2 shows the completed grid for this particular case study.

The 'wow' factor – or the secret ingredient in information literacy teaching

However serious the business of teaching information literacy is, there is something to be said for using a tool like Zotero to 'wow' a group into wanting to learn more! Jason Puckett, author of one of the best books I have

Target audience				
Format				
Learning outcomes	Information literacy outcomes		Faculty-specific learning goals	
Contributor focus	Library staff	Other	Other	Other
Planning, activities and timings	Activities			Timings
Learning styles and related preparation	Activist	Pragmatist	Theorist	Reflector
Reflection planned (attendees)				
Evaluation of teaching				

Figure 6.1 *Planning grid (Teaching Programmes English Faculty Library)*

come across on using Zotero, refers to this 'wow factor' (Puckett, 2011). How do I see this applying in our workshops? Sometimes you know something vaguely, but would be hard pressed to say why you do nothing about it; for example a student may realize that they should find a method for improving their time management, but fail to do so. It's almost as if you, or they, have acquired some knowledge and understanding in a generalist way but it doesn't have much effect. And then one day the penny drops. What was elusive and possibly unimportant becomes fascinating and worthy of consideration.

On a recent trip to Venice I encountered this scenario. Played out, it amounted to knowing, in the way that we all accumulate bits and pieces of information, that Leonardo da Vinci was important in Renaissance Italy. A chance visit to an exhibition that I almost didn't bother with (the entrance was hidden by a dull curtain, and it cost eight euros to get into) transformed me from being vaguely bored by an historical figure to entranced by the unbelievable cleverness of the man. How did this happen? In this particular

Target audience	• Postgraduates, academics of the Faculty, promoted as equally good for teaching as research. • This focus on the tool and what it allows a researcher to do means that the audience can be wide-ranging. The underlying assumption is that the tool is either not familiar at all, or will have been tried and rejected previously for some reason, or the user is facing a problem with using it, or may simply have not considered the wider uses for which the tool can be used.		
Format	Workshop; presentations and demos first, break-out groups and discussion to follow.		
Learning outcomes	**Main learning outcomes** • An overview of the need to manage information and how one particular tool – Zotero – might assist with this. • Through demonstrations and follow-up peer-to-peer coaching and help in the workshop, give those attending a clear idea of *how* Zotero is used, and *what* it can be used for. • Ensure that everyone attending, who wishes, is able to set up Zotero and use it, download citations and create libraries for themselves, understand Zotero's searching, bibliography creation and cite-while-you-write functionalities. • Attendees to evaluate the tool against their current practice and consider what further action they may take.		**Faculty-specific learning goals for graduates** • Bibliographical skills • Generic research skills (project management, record management, etc.) • IT – electronic resources; bibliographical and other database software • Publication, including articles, book to thesis (Faculty of English Graduate Training Programme, 2012)
Contributor focus	**Library staff** An overview of Zotero set within the context of the need to manage information.	**Other (academic)** Demonstrate their current use of Zotero; explain their choice of the tool and how it informs their research practice. Discuss problems with using this specific tool. Demonstrate the basics of downloading material into Zotero ('wow' factor).	**Other (postgraduate)** Demonstrate their current use of Zotero with reference to the reason for their choice of the tool and rationale for using it. How it informs their research and teaching work. Specifically looks at the creation of text with footnotes and bibliography, type of material stored and searching capability, Zotero groups for student reading lists ('wow' factor).

Figure 6.2 *Planning grid for Managing Information (Zotero Workshop) (Teaching Programmes English Faculty Library, pages 75 and 76) (continued overleaf)*

Planning, activities and timings	Activities			Timings
	• Intro overview (Prezi [http://prezi.com])			5 mins
	• Demo (Academic)			10 mins
	• Demo (Postgraduate)			10–15 mins
	• Workshop with Academic, Postgraduate, Librarian, Computer Officer to answer queries and work alongside attendees using and discussing the tool			20 mins
	• Review discussion with all led by a facilitator to draw together experiences, queries, review of the tool			5–10 mins
	• Final evaluation using Poll Everywhere [www.polleverywhere.com] – send a simple text comment assessing impact of the tool and next step			5 mins
Learning styles and related preparation	**Activist**	**Pragmatist**	**Theorist**	**Reflector**
	Hands on tasks without it being a threatening activity, using their own laptop in small group; opportunity to use mobile phones for evaluation.	Key advertising of the event to demonstrate that learning Zotero will save them time, increase the quality of their work; workshop style which allows them to get on with trialling Zotero for a purpose, so important to set up the 'workshop time' with a structure and purpose.	Information given in advance allows them to find Zotero in advance and check it out, link to the website for additional help in advance; learning outcomes specifically stated in advertising and at the beginning of the session; handouts given out as they come in; handouts to leave with all key information from the Prezi; a how to get started; a comparison with Endnote and how it all sits within the management of information. Make sure that there is a handout showing how to use Zotero for teaching purposes as well. Add all information to CamTools (local VLE) and e-mail out links.	Information given in advance allows them to find Zotero in advance and check it out, link to the website for additional help in advance; learning outcomes specifically stated; not required to actively participate in hands on session but can just look over a shoulder; opportunity to reflect in closing discussion and opportunity to contribute in Poll Everywhere. Reflection continues with handouts and a follow up e-mail to all who attended asking for feedback on how they are getting along.
Reflection planned (attendees)	• Before the group workshop time, establish range of experience of Zotero from: never tried it, novice, used for awhile, comfortable, pretty expert. During the group workshop time facilitate peer-to-peer discussions of the pros and cons of the tool. Use peer knowledge of other similar tools to weigh up and assess the usefulness of Zotero.			
	• Complete the session with discussion to address issues from the trial time and use Poll Everywhere for a quick straw poll on what people intend to do next.			
	• Follow-up evaluation with attendees after the event with the offer of more help.			
Evaluation of teaching	Peer-to-peer evaluation; discussion with other contributors following the event; evaluation of what next to be included			
	Attendee evaluation: e-mail survey to attendees			

Figure 6.2 (continued)

exhibition, many of the drawings in da Vinci's notebooks had been made into models – not just to look at, but to play with and experiment with. To me, the man is now a genius, and I'm hooked and intrigued by what he did, and want to know more.

It struck me forcibly that the process I went through is not dissimilar to the ones we may find facing us in our teaching. What transformed my own personal engagement with Leonardo da Vinci was the hands-on exhibition that suited my personal learning style. What I see time and time again with varying levels and groups of students is that the 'wow' factor in seeing what Zotero can do provides a perfect opportunity to engage the students, 'wows' them, and thereby creates the right climate for learning.

Conclusion

My reflection on the workshops that we run at the Faculty of English is that they work because we are all learning together. There is often a 'wow' factor involved as someone discovers, shares and teaches the rest of us something we didn't know, and actually it doesn't always matter if we don't manage to cover everything we planned – but it is in how we deal with the subject of managing information that we inspire others to engage and reflect on what they do and to make informed decisions about what they do, how they do it, and why they do it.

Bibliography

Hart, S., Dixon, A., Drummond, M. J. and McIntyre, D. (2004) *Learning without Limits*, Open University Press.

Honey, P. and Mumford, A. (2000) *The Learning Styles Helper's Guide*, Peter Honey Publications.

Kolb, D. A. (1984) *Experiential Learning: experience as the source of learning and development*, Prentice-Hall.

Puckett, J. (2011) *Zotero: a guide for librarians, researchers and educators*, Association of College and Research Libraries.

Tilley, E. (2012) *Zotero Workshop* [Prezi], http://prezi.com/8o015yqhsspa/zotero-workshop/.

Strand Seven

The ethical dimension of information

Lyn Parker

Where Strand Three aims to articulate, explore and develop the academic literacies of reading and writing within the student's disciplinary context, Strand Seven builds upon these competences to explore ethical values around information use. This includes 'need-to-know' issues such as referencing and attribution, plagiarism, copyright and intellectual property guidelines; however, it also opens the way for rich discussion around where the borderline between bad scholarship and unethical or illegal behaviour lies. This approach creates opportunities for students to move beyond black-and-white usage guidelines and towards an informed and nuanced appreciation of the ethics of information.

Lyn is Secretary of the CILIP Information Literacy group and a member of the Universities UK (UUK) Copyright Working Group. She took part in the ANCIL expert consultation which helped inform and shape the final curriculum. Specializing in copyright, intellectual property and learning and teaching developments at Sheffield University, Lyn's expertise in the ethical aspects of information literacy made her the natural choice for a Strand Seven case study.

Institutional context

The University of Sheffield is in the Top Ten of the Russell Group of leading research-intensive universities and was named 'University of the Year' 2011 in the *Times Higher Education* awards. The priority themes of the university's Learning and Teaching Strategy 2011–16 include internationalization, employability, research-led learning and developing communities of learning.[1] The University Library has aligned its Strategic Plan and Objectives[2] with those of the university. Within Learning and Teaching, the aim is to work in close partnership with departments to embed information literacy into the curriculum while engaging students in an understanding of their transferable skills. The university has the aspiration that all Sheffield students should be information literate when they graduate. Faculty librarians liaise with course leaders to design appropriate activities and assessment to ensure this is achieved.

This case study reflects on various projects at the university which come under the heading of ethical use of information. It starts with the development of an online plagiarism tutorial and quiz, which supports the university's Unfair Means policy and guidance; shows the need for increased copyright awareness among both staff and students, and how this has been achieved through the development of a Copyright Hub, bringing together guidance from various departments within the University; and finally reflects on the Digital Footprint project, which seeks to ensure that students can use social media and the internet to enhance their employability while maintaining their e-safety and privacy.

Information literacy development at the University of Sheffield

Information literacy at the University of Sheffield is aligned with SCONUL's Seven Pillars model, originally developed in 1999 and since revised in 2011 (SCONUL, 1999; 2011). The emphasis when delivering information literacy sessions has developed over time and the focus has shifted from 'construct search strategies for locating' and 'locate and access' to 'compare and evaluate' and 'organize, apply and communicate' and even more recently to 'synthesize and create'. It is these higher-order capabilities, which include critical thinking, evaluation, synthesis, communication and knowledge creation, that should be the key focus for any development activity. The University Library has long delivered information literacy sessions organized in partnership with departments and tailored to the needs of particular groups of students. This work was enhanced through the development of a suite of online information literacy tutorials in 2004.

The development of the Information Skills Resource stemmed from a project called LibCT, to investigate how to embed Library Services into WebCT, the new virtual learning environment (VLE) being rolled out to the university at the time (see Stubley, 2005). Stubley found that e-learning champions wanted seamless access to library materials from within their VLE courses, including online reading lists, digitized course readings, information literacy training and enquiry services. Various projects were set up in the library to meet these needs and eventually came together to form a 'library toolkit'.

Through a Learning and Teaching Development Grant a centrally maintained information skills resource was created for use by all students at the university, initially delivered through WebCT. At the time, the library wished to address three specific needs through the information skills resource to:

- provide all undergraduate students with easy and flexible access to important information skills materials from within the VLE
- enter into a dialogue with academic departments that would lead to embedding information skills fully in their teaching and make it part of the formal assessment;
- enable the selection of elements of the generic resource so that they can be embedded into subject-specific VLE-based course material and modified to suit particular information skills needs.

The library named the resource the Information Skills Resource rather than the Information Literacy Resource, as the term information literacy was not widely used at that time within the university. This position changed rapidly with the success of our Centre for Excellence in Teaching and Learning (CETL) bid and the establishment of CILASS, the Centre for Inquiry-based Learning in the Arts and Social Sciences, closely followed by the launch of the Learning and Teaching Strategy 2005–10 and the development of the Sheffield Graduate Award.

Initially the library worked with Biomedical Science, Law and Nursing and Midwifery to test embedding learning objects within subject specific courses and with Human Communication Sciences to test the generic resource (Parker and Freeman, 2005). The iSchool was also involved as part of the Project Steering Group. The resource was developed in WebCT Campus but very soon after was incorporated into WebCT Vista, and more recently into Blackboard Learn. Figure 7.1 illustrates the home page of the original resource. The library has been included in pilots each time the university has migrated its VLE to a new platform. The resource now has material available

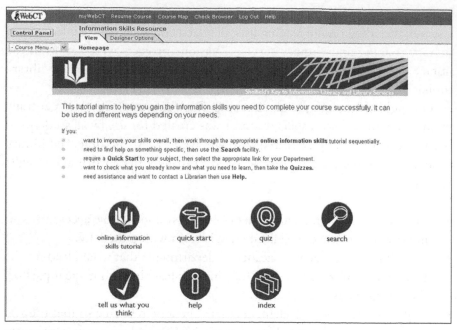

Figure 7.1 *Home page for the original Information Skills Resource*

for each of the 50 departments; the minimum offered is a Quick Start for subject resources, a referencing tutorial and a guide to their key database, as well as generic tutorials on Effective Searching, Searching StarPlus, the library's new catalogue, Using Other Libraries and several other topics. It has also been expanded to include material aimed at postgraduate research students to support the Doctoral Development Programme. The library continues to work on the basis that impact on students' results is greatest through integration and contextualization, and firmly embedding information literacy in their studies.

CILASS and the Sheffield Graduate

Funding was awarded in 2005 to establish CILASS, one of the Centres for Excellence in Teaching and Learning. Inquiry-based learning (IBL) was promoted as an approach to 'involve students in collaborative discipline-based and inter-disciplinary inquiries, develop their information literacy capabilities, and use information and communications technologies imaginatively to enhance the learning experience' (McKinney and Levy, 2006). Projects were developed to combine research experience with practical workshop activities while using technology to enhance collaborative group work. The establishment of CILASS, the strong partnership between the iSchool and the University Library and the ongoing work to embed information literacy in the curriculum all impacted strategically at the institutional level. The university's Learning, Teaching and Assessment Strategy (2005–10) contained an explicit commitment to both IBL and IL, highlighting the capacity for students to:

- carry out extended independent inquiry, formulating relevant questions and engaging critically with a wide range of evidence
- demonstrate the core capabilities and skills of information literacy, interacting confidently with the nature and structure of information in their subject and handling information in a professional and ethical manner.

Indeed, in the latest Learning and Teaching Strategy (2011–16) the characteristics of the Sheffield Graduate[3] have been updated and information literacy is recognized as discrete from skill in the use of IT. Each academic department is required to formulate a departmental-level learning and teaching strategy and review annually how they are working towards achieving the university's objectives. The library is able, through the faculty librarians, to influence this strategic thinking.

Unfair means and plagiarism

Originally individual departmental referencing tutorials within the Information Skills Resource included a section on plagiarism, partly to answer the question 'why should I bother with referencing correctly?' However, in 2007 a Working Group of the University's Quality and Standards Sub-Committee was established to:

- consider whether the university is taking sufficient steps to minimize opportunities for plagiarism to occur
- ensure that appropriate procedures are in place to deal fairly and consistently with students suspected of plagiarism, and that staff and students are made aware of these procedures

- ensure that appropriate guidance and support is in place to assist departments in promoting good academic practice.

The issues that lead students to plagiarize were discussed, and the action required at departmental and institutional level to ensure good practice and a consistent and fair approach was defined and allocated. The University Library was represented on the Group and tasked with providing a separate online plagiarism tutorial and quiz, which could be used either for formative or summative assessment.

The recommendations of the Group relevant to this case study were as follows:

1   The term 'unfair means' should be used as an umbrella term for plagiarism, buying or commissioning assignments, self-plagiarism, collusion and fabrication.
2   Compulsory study skills sessions should be provided for all new students; they should include understanding plagiarism, referencing and good academic practice. There should be at least one face-to-face taught session for all students provided by the department, which should be supplemented by further taught sessions and/or electronic tutorials. For programmes lasting more than a year, there should be refresher sessions in subsequent years.
3   Study skills tutorials should be embedded in departmental modules, so that they are perceived by students as part of the programme.
4   Support from the library on developing information literacy, including the web-based plagiarism tutorial and support for referencing skills, should be taken up by departments across the university.
5   Departments should reduce the opportunities to plagiarize and give consideration to the use of a variety of assessment tasks. Requesting submission of pieces of self-reflection, submission of drafts or portfolios of learning would also be useful.
6   Workshops should be organized for academic staff to promote examples of good practice for study skills etc.

The plagiarism tutorial (see Figure 7.2) was developed over the summer of 2007 and reviewed by faculty members on the Working Group as well as Student Services to ensure that it conformed to the institutional policy and

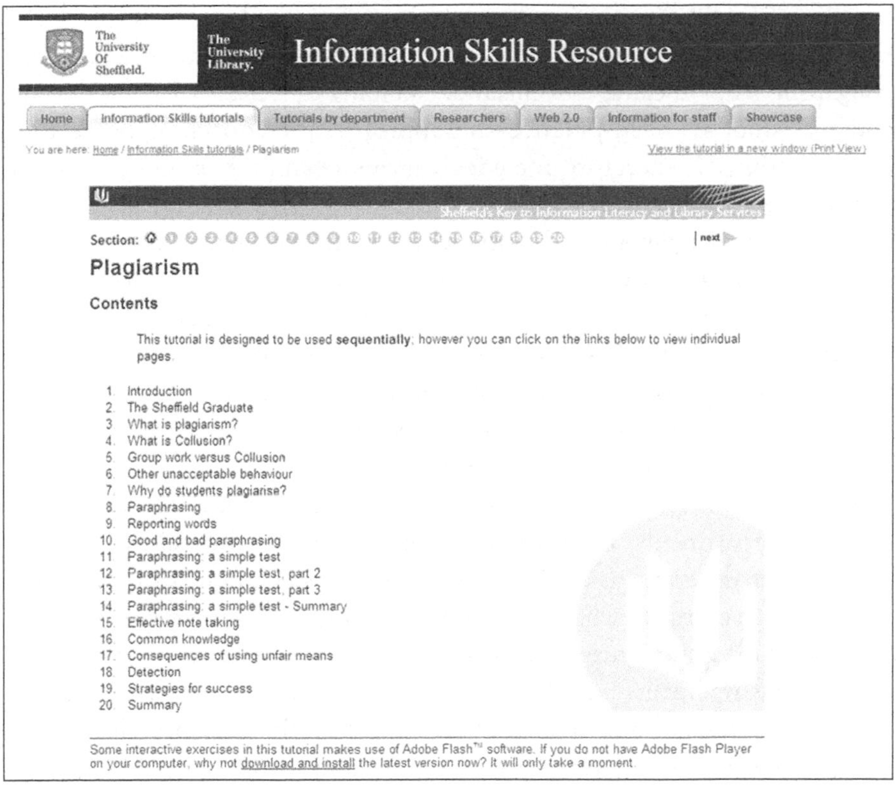

Figure 7.2 *Plagiarism tutorial*

met individual departmental needs. The quiz was set up within the VLE and academics could request for it to be uploaded into individual modules as necessary. Since 2007, the tutorial has undergone various updates, most notably in 2010 to include guidance relevant to postgraduate research students when the compulsory submission of PhDs as e-theses was made mandatory, and in 2011 when the Unfair Means guidance and departmental actions were updated to include 'aiding and abetting'. The original quiz was developed with ten questions but in 2008 permission was given by Nottingham Trent University to use the questions from the Plagiarism Badger resource[4] and increase the Question Bank to 20 questions. The intention is to collaborate with other universities interested in developing a Question Bank for information literacy, including the ethical use of information, plagiarism, copyright, intellectual property and data protection (Griffiths, 2010).

The tutorial was written for a student audience and its design was heavily based on Carroll's work, with some of the exercises from her book turned into interactive exercises (Carroll, 2007). It is based on the premise that most plagiarism is not cheating but misunderstanding or misuse of paraphrasing, and that students need practice and appropriate feedback to check their understanding. It therefore includes various examples of good and bad paraphrasing and the use of quotes. The tutorial also promotes the need for good time management and note-taking to the students. The need for consistency of approach is covered, and showing authority of sources and validity of argument, being able to trace references and evidencing the broad research behind the assignment are emphasized. The tutorial was benchmarked against offerings from other universities, including that from the University of Leeds,[5] which was subsequently highly commended in the Jorum learning and teaching competition.

In practice the plagiarism tutorial and quiz are used in a variety of ways by different departments. Discussion on integrating the tutorial has led to a dialogue with departments on the way they support students to avoid plagiarism and reference correctly, which system they use and why, and how they convey to students the importance of their finding their own voice when writing (not only putting arguments into their own words but developing their opinions). Each of the library's referencing tutorials matches the guidance given in the module handbooks so that consistent information is conveyed through every avenue. For example, in the Department of Town and Regional Planning the liaison librarian delivers a workshop to first-year students within weeks 1 and 2 of the first semester. The session covers basic library skills, referencing and how to avoid plagiarism. The students use the online tutorials in class with the librarian facilitating the session. They are then set a library skills quiz and the plagiarism quiz as summative work forming 20% of the module mark (see Figure 7.3). Students are encouraged to have a second window open while completing the quizzes and look up the answers or revise the tutorial. They are given two attempts and have access to feedback on individual questions after the first attempt. The focus is on learning rather than catching students out!

The Department of Automatic Control and Systems Engineering (ACSE) delivers a lecture to its first year students in week 1 which covers report writing, referencing and avoiding plagiarism and collusion. Plagiarism and collusion are then discussed in personal tutorials using realistic examples to clarify any misconceptions they might have. The online tutorial (see Figure 7.4) is available in the VLE to all students in ACSE, and after the lecture and

Figure 7.3 *Department of Town and Regional Planning tutorial*

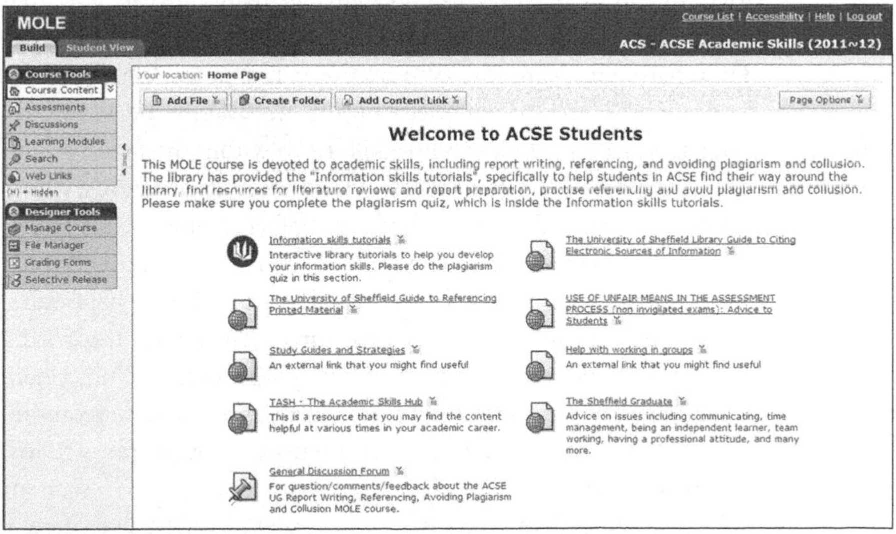

Figure 7.4 *Department of Automatic Control and Systems Engineering tutorial*

the personal tutorials students are expected to complete the online quiz. The tutorial is also used for revision purposes to remind students at the start of each academic year the need for the ethical use of information.

The tutorial is also used within the university in individual cases which involve poor academic practice rather than unfair means, or where there is insufficient evidence to proceed. The student will be provided with additional support and required to show evidence that they have worked through the study material provided. The usage statistics show that Avoiding Plagiarism is one of the most heavily used of all the library tutorials (24,376 hits in the academic year 2009–10), the others being the referencing tutorials. Links are provided from Student Services Advice, the Students Union, Learning and Teaching Services advice for tutors as well as the library pages. It can be regarded as totally embedded within the institution.

Copyright awareness

The issues surrounding plagiarism often overlap with those of copyright and intellectual property. In the world of Web 2.0 and increasing use of social media within learning and teaching, when 'cut/copy and paste' is so easy and the culture of sharing is so engrained, clear copyright guidelines and an embedded educational awareness programme are essential for both staff and students. Copyright can be regarded as central to virtually every activity that the university undertakes, whether research, teaching, outreach or commercial enterprise. Therefore, an awareness of copyright law is not only part of ensuring our graduates are information literate in their ethical use of information, but an essential employability skill. Both within their studies and eventually in the world of work, students will encounter situations where copyright has been outstripped by the affordances of emerging technologies, or where the issues are so complex that decisions are not clear-cut and must be based on an assessment of the risk of litigation. This is already happening at the university with the use of lecture capture technology, the media streaming service, the development of the university's Enterprise Unit, where students are encouraged to set up their own businesses, the mandate requiring the deposit of all PhD theses and the production of websites, videos, podcasts, screen-casts, or a combination of which form part of student assessment. Changes in academic practice, often related to the use of new technology to enhance learning, mean that everyone at the university needs an understanding of basic copyright and an awareness of where they can seek advice.

No one section of the University of Sheffield has overall responsibility for copyright. The University Library offers advice on third-party copyright material, administers the Copyright Licensing Agency licence and copyright compliance for that, and negotiates the licences for electronic journals and databases. Research and Innovation Services provide guidance on intellectual property, help commercialize research and negotiate contracts on behalf of staff. Computing Services (CICS) deal with all reports of university computing facilities being used to copy or distribute copyright material without authorization of the copyright owner and manage the use of the VLE and emerging technologies.

Increasingly, enquiries have become more complex and blurred between the domains of first party and third party, between educational and commercial use, and between the individual's rights and those of the university. In the light of these issues, a paper presented initially to the Learning and Teaching Committee and subsequently endorsed by the University Executive Board outlined the need to develop a central hub at the top level of the university website, drawing together the university guidance and policy and making clear to both staff and students their individual responsibility to abide by copyright law and regulations. The University Library is responsible for the general copyright guidelines (Figure 7.5) and 'Copyright in an Online Environment' (Figure 7.6) and these pages

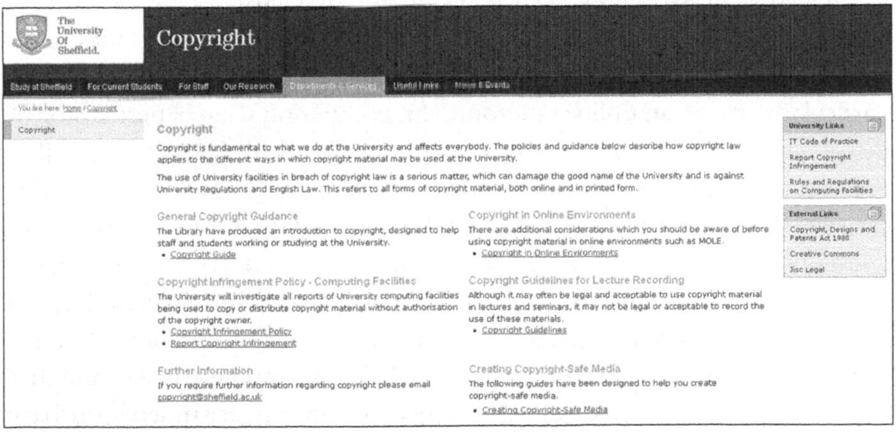

Figure 7.5 *General copyright guidelines*

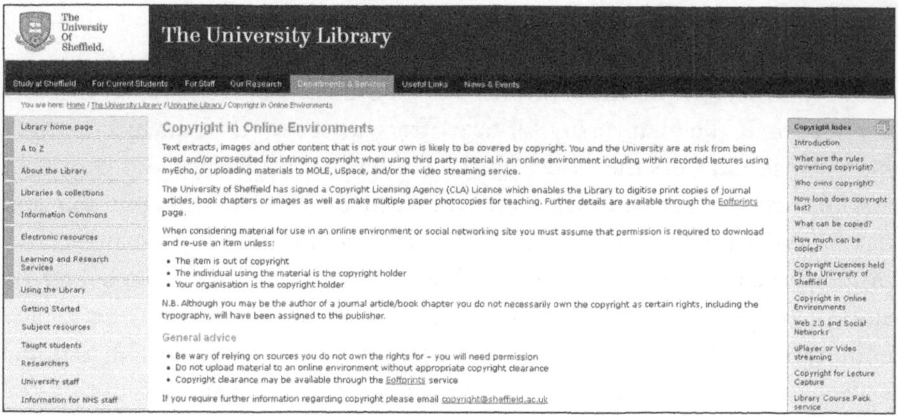

Figure 7.6 *Copyright in online environments*

(www.shef.ac.uk/copyright) were totally reviewed and updated as part of the project. The work has been endorsed and commended by the Learning and Teaching Committee and publicity of its availability both internally and externally is ongoing.

Work has now moved on to providing an educational programme, initially with academic staff but with the aim to produce workshops and activities suitable for students. The session delivered to learning technologists was most effective in disseminating the guidance, as they are responsible for rolling out the new VLE, Blackboard Learn, and training staff within individual departments in its implementation. This work has led to further workshops for individual departments, such as the School of Education, and groups of staff, including librarians. The outline for the workshop is flexible but follows an IBL delivery style. There is a short introduction covering basic copyright, particularly within an online environment, comparing what is permissible in face-to-face sessions as opposed to online. Typical scenarios are then presented and attendees are asked for their opinion of what they think they can do. The scenarios are gathered beforehand from frequently asked questions or specific requests. This is followed up with an open question and answer discussion and a debate on recent copyright issues, including the Hargreaves review and copyright licences such as Creative Commons. The group of staff who worked on the Copyright Hub continue to meet and their current aim is to produce guidance aimed specifically at students on basic copyright within a Web 2.0 environment.

Digital Footprint

The Digital Footprint project has come about from a discussion around the need for students to protect their privacy and understand other people's copyright and their own intellectual property, while developing responsible use of social media and promoting their own online presence to potential employers. Staff and students need an awareness of what their profile and data says about them, what information is being collected about them and how to develop a professional face as well as a social one. From a careers perspective they need to be able to seek out information about potential employers and understand how social media is being used in workplaces. The project is still at the scoping stage and initially involves the University Library, Careers Service, the University of Sheffield Enterprise Unit and CICS. The aim is to produce learning resources aimed at academic staff with teaching materials and suggested activities to use with their students on the range of topics shown in Table 7.1.

Table 7.1 *Digital Footprint project*

Publishing	Networking	Legal responsibilities
Using rich media	Social media	Intellectual property right
Creating a web presence	Blogging	Ethics
Online discourse	Professional networks	Copyright
Search engines and metadata	Social online networks	First party
	Alerts and mentions	Third party
Professional and personal identities	Employability and job seeking	Creative Commons
	Online reputation	Moral rights
	Privacy	Avoiding plagiarism

The templates would include open educational content and case studies of best practice within the university and other higher education institutions as well as newly written material as required. As with the work on copyright awareness, endorsement is being sought from senior management and it is planned to integrate it in the new e-learning strategy being written at present.

Conclusions

These case studies highlight the latest work at the University of Sheffield on the ethical dimension of information. The University Library is seeking to embed information literacy into the curriculum at an institutional level. Progress has been achieved by working with senior personnel to seek their endorsement of the principles and gain the attention of course leaders within departments. Even with top-level approval, individual lecturers respond to these initiatives in various ways, from enthusiasm and adoption to conservatism and resistance. Therefore, embedding information literacy in the curriculum requires a flexible approach, a range of strategies and an open dialogue between the various stakeholders. The broader the remit of information literacy to encompass all areas of the information landscape, the wider the range of stakeholders becomes. Real-world examples should be employed to put the need into context and make it relevant to other key university objectives demanding management's attention: employability, internationalization, research-led learning, retention, etc. Individual academics need to see this relevance not only to the university strategy and departmental learning and teaching requirements but also to their own particular discipline; they need to have a sense of ownership of any generic central resource or library input to reinforce the learning outcomes and ensure student engagement. Student engagement is more likely if provision is set in context and forms part of their community of learning (Wenger, 1998).

The original design of the Information Skills Resource was based on the work of McAvinia and Oliver. They researched four models for the way skills can be incorporated into courses from a central provision (McAvinia and Oliver, 2002, 213):

1   **Optional model:** materials are recommended by tutors/course documents but the student is left to search them out and use them at their own discretion; no formal training is provided and there is no formal relationship with specific parts of the course.
2   **Directed model:** materials are recommended by tutors/course documents and students get formal introduction/training in their use and are directed to them from time to time, but they are not strongly identified with specific parts of the course.
3   **Integrated model:** materials are recommended, formal introduction is provided, students are directed to materials at appropriate points of the course and tutors associate materials with course/module delivery.
4   **Contextualized model:** materials are recommended and training

provided; students are directed to use materials at appropriate points and tutors contextualize the materials for use in their course.

McAvinia and Oliver showed that to be effective, generic study skills materials must be integrated and contextualized. This was confirmed by the original evaluation of the Information Skills Resource (Parker and Freeman, 2005), and continues to form the principles behind the information literacy policy. Thus, a greater impact on students' results is achieved when information literacy is firmly embedded into the course, when the academic emphasizes the importance to the students and reinforces the context and relevance for their studies. The librarians, therefore, continue to advocate that information literacy needs to be blended into the learning process.

Notes

1   www.sheffield.ac.uk/lets/staff/lts.
2   www.sheffield.ac.uk/library/about/strategicplan.
3   www.shef.ac.uk/sheffieldgraduate/students.
4   www.ntu.ac.uk/llr/developing_skills/referencing_plagiarism.
5   www.ldu.leeds.ac.uk/plagiarism.

Bibliography

Carroll, J. (2007) *A Handbook for Deterring Plagiarism in Higher Education*, 2nd edn, Oxford Centre for Staff and Learning Development.

Griffiths, J. (2010) *Building the IL Question Bank*, www.informationliteracy.org.uk/2010/10/uk-online-information-literacy-assessment-question-bank/.

McAvinia, C. and Oliver, M. (2002) 'But My Subject's Different': a web-based approach to supporting disciplinary lifelong learning skills, *Computers and Education*, **38**, 1–3, 209–20.

McKinney, P. and Levy, P. (2006) Inquiry-Based Learning and Information Literacy Development: a CETL approach, *ITALICS* **5** (1), www.ics.heacademy.ac.uk/italics/vol5iss2.htm.

Parker, L. and Freeman, M. (2005) Blended Learning: a mutual approach to embedding information literacy into the curriculum, www.lilacconference.com/dw/archive/resources/2005/parker.pdf.

SCONUL (2011) *The Seven Pillars of Information Literacy*,
   www.sconul.ac.uk/groups/information_literacy/seven_pillars.html.
SCONUL Information Skills Task Force (1999) *Information Skills in Higher Education: a SCONUL position paper prepared by the SCONUL Advisory Committee on Information Literacy*,
   www.sconul.ac.uk/groups/information_literacy/papers/seven_pillars.html.
Stubley, P. (2005) Just One Piece of the Jigsaw: e-literacy in the wider perspective. In: Melling, M. (ed.), *Supporting E-learning: a guide for library and information managers*, Facet Publishing.
Wenger, E. (1998) *Communities of Practice: learning, meaning and identity*, Cambridge University Press.

Strand Eight

Presenting and communicating knowledge

Andy Priestner

Strand Eight covers all aspects of presenting and communicating knowledge – one of the less traditional aspects of information literacy, but also probably one of the most important in terms of a transferable and life skill. This strand includes finding your voice, learning to use language appropriately in academic and other types of writing, and using evidence to justify a position. In a digital environment how you present yourself and manage your online identity is an increasingly important facet of information literacy. This includes an awareness of how you appear to others online, deciding on an appropriate level of information to communicate with different audiences, managing your 'digital footprint' and evaluating the suitability of different locations and tools for presenting your online presence. The strand also includes an understanding of how to communicate appropriately, choosing appropriate writing styles and formats for a specific audience, as well as understanding the methods of publishing research in your discipline and the relationship between writing style, audience and publication platform.

Andy was another member of the expert group consulted during the ANCIL research to provide input into both how to teach the curriculum and what to include in it. Strand Eight of the curriculum focuses on how to present and communicate knowledge in the broadest sense, and in many institutions teaching these skills has fallen outside the responsibility of librarians. However, the two examples of teaching sessions from Judge Business School show how librarians are often pioneering and leading the way in terms of being advocates of social media. Andy's approach also highlights the subtle but important shift from teacher to facilitator of learning, and the importance of allowing students to be active in the learning process.

Institutional context

Judge Business School is a leading provider of innovative and practical business and management education to executives, graduates and undergraduates. It is a fully integrated department of the University of Cambridge and boasts a world-class faculty of 50 members, many of whom are leaders in their field. In 2011 it was ranked second in the UK and seventh globally for one-year MBA programmes by the *Financial Times*. Our flagship MBA and Masters in Finance programmes have course fees of £36–38,000 per annum.

Given this context of high-calibre members and equally high expectations of levels of service, Information and Library Services staff put much thought and deliberation into the design and delivery of teaching sessions. Although we also support doctoral candidates, researchers and faculty, our principal learners are students on very intensive one-year postgraduate courses and this naturally impacts on our approach to teaching. In a nutshell, we aim to make our sessions sensitive to their time constraints, relevant to those attending, and scheduled in line with tight timetables.

Although I would not anticipate rolling out the full ANCIL model here, because of the constraints described above and the fact that the vast majority of our students are postgraduates, many of the strands are very relevant in terms of their content and approach. During the past six months I have presented sessions under the ANCIL framework with a view to testing its relevance and value. This has resulted in a more systematic and measured approach to course design and the results have been very promising. I have selected two of the sessions I have recently delivered as examples of teaching on Strand Eight, entitled 'Twitter for Research' and 'The Value of Blogging'.

Aim of the sessions

Although I would argue that social media are not crucial to the success of any of our students in terms of their assignment marks, or indeed to the overall endeavours of our PhDs and faculty, how you present yourself and manage your online identity has, of course, become a very important consideration for everyone, and having positioned library staff as experts in the field we are now regularly asked for advice and tips. However, as with every component of the information literacy spectrum, the majority of our users do not seem to be thinking enough about this area, particularly in terms of the opportunities that social media could offer to enhance their online presence, reputation and networks, provided that critical judgements are made around voice, style and platform.

In respect of the Twitter session the intention was to offer reliable up-to-date information about why using this platform is a valid and appropriate channel when engaged in academic research. Other key objectives were to tackle persistent media stereotypes (e.g. it's just for celebrities telling you what they had for their breakfast and is therefore a waste of time), and to highlight the many possible applications and benefits (e.g. keeping current in your field, connecting with experts) derived from maintaining a Twitter presence. The blogging session was also intended to open the eyes of attendees to the possibilities inherent in that activity and more specifically to encourage them to consider its value as a means of developing and honing one's academic voice, and recording and analysing experiences, concepts and theories relevant to their research.

Both sessions sought more broadly to combat a perceived institutional reluctance to take social media forward, and seriously, in its many forms. There was also a definite element of library advocacy in electing to offer these sessions, demonstrating that the library is keeping up with new technologies and far more than just a physical space containing books.

Developing the sessions

Although most of the teaching delivered by the Information and Library Services at Judge Business School is developed for specific courses at specific times, embedded into the curriculum to ensure relevance and compulsory in order to maximize attendance, for these social media sessions I took a different tack. As these platforms have conceivable benefit to all members of Judge I took the rare step of opening up these sessions to the entire School community. I believed that this would not only encourage cross-pollination of ideas and reactions during the session but also help attendees to see the possibilities of social media from very different and equally valid perspectives at whatever point they were at in their academic career. This in turn meant that rather than trying to develop a session that was generically relevant to everyone, I would seek to focus on different aspects and experiences that would strike a chord with different attendees at different points.

I also decided that the sessions should be exploratory rather than a 'how-to', although I made sure that library staff were promoted in the session as a source of help for the practical next steps should the session prompt the attendee to find out more about blogging and/or micro-blogging. Having said this, in the case of the Twitter session, the 'how-to' is a key means of describing the value of the platform, so inevitably some examples ventured more towards this practical territory.

While I usually pursue a more constructivist pedagogical approach in my teaching, these sessions could only go so far along that road. In the Twitter session especially there was a definite need to instruct and advise, didactically at times, on practical applications and benefits. However, I was very careful to make the point that with social media, value is very much a personal matter arrived at over time as the 'ins and outs' of a new technology are learned. This is not to say that the sessions were traditionally or wholly didactic, as there was an intention to engage through audience questions and active encouragement to share experience.

During their planning I started to see the sessions as springboards to new ideas and experiences, a catalyst which could encourage attendees to find out more and learn more for themselves.

Collaboration

My hope was to present both sessions described above collaboratively with colleagues from the Business School, being sold on the benefits of such an approach: the fact that collaboration enables the offering of different perspectives, levels of expertise and experiences; the draw of having different presenters of status (in reality an academic is often more of a draw than a librarian and they can often have the effect of legitimizing the session in the eyes of their students); and the stark fact that if you don't like how, or what, one speaker is saying then the other presenters might be more to your taste.

Unfortunately, for the Twitter session I only received two responses to my open request to faculty and students for a co-teacher. One was from a researcher who has been examining Twitter in respect of earthquake risk but hadn't used it much as a networking tool – I decided that he should have a guest spot to take the session down a different route as an example of an interesting practical application. The other response was from a researcher whose offer I respectfully declined, as she had been using Twitter to research the weekly outcome of the television talent show *The X Factor*, which I felt sounded too populist in approach and might have strengthened rather than diluted the belief that Twitter is a waste of time. This lack of co-presenters meant that the session would not be as balanced, or perhaps as authoritative, as I'd hoped, but at the same time confirmed that there was a definite need for it if there were so few exponents out there.

The blogging session was, conversely, blessed with a total of five co-presenters, with a volunteering PhD student, faculty member (the Director of the Master of Finance programme, no less) and a member of support staff, as well as myself and another information and library colleague. All were asked to present on why they started blogging and the value they placed on the activity, with an emphasis on personal experience. In fact, presenters were encouraged to 'story-tell', given that this a very effective means of engaging audience and expressing meaning.

Format, platform, duration and frequency

The format for both sessions was of a lecture-cum-discussion with an informal, and intentionally exploratory, 'I/we may not have all the answers', tone. For the Twitter session, a Prezi (http://prezi.com) formed the backbone of the session with high-image content and embedded videos to add flavour, colour and impact. Prezi is web-based presentation software that has a less linear approach than traditional presentation packages. The Prezi (see Figure 8.1) was deliberately designed as a standalone learning object, which could inform and entertain non-attendees – an aim which seems to have been very successfully achieved as, at the last count, it has been viewed over 4200 times. There was also a live demonstration of HootSuite (www.hootsuite.com) in order to see Twitter in action and present the possibility of search alerts and different lists and channels beyond the vanilla Twitter.com interface. The session was also live-tweeted by one of my team so, appropriately, also reached an audience beyond the room.

For the blogging session, presenters in the main elected to use their blog as a backdrop to what they wanted to say to, and share with, the audience. In both sessions, questions were asked and taken throughout. In the case of the latter there was designated plenary discussion at the end for further questions and observations to be raised and responded to. It is worth mentioning that in the case of both sessions a hands-on workshop was considered at first,

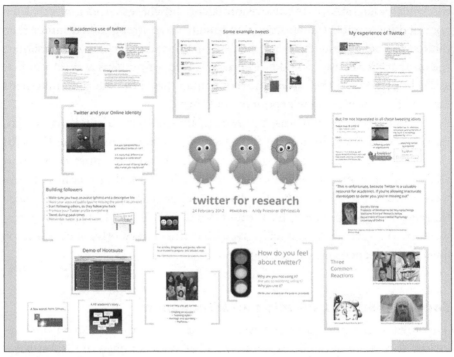

Figure 8.1 *The Twitter Prezi*

but becasue of the probable mix of skills and preferences in the invited audience – e.g. faculty being much less keen on hands-on than students – and the decision to go with exploration rather than practical nuts and bolts, the idea was dropped, although hands-on follow-up instruction was offered.

In order to encourage attendance both sessions were billed as a digestible 45 minutes rather than an hour, and empty timeslots for students, faculty and staff were selected using course timetables. Both sessions ran for an hour in the end, but this was intentional. There are plans to run both sessions again in due course as many members were unable to attend. As a direct result of the Twitter session, I have since delivered practical hands-on and advanced Twitter sessions to faculty and students on getting started on Twitter, building followers and 'finding your Twitter voice'.

Learning outcomes

The specific learning outcomes for the sessions were: increased awareness of online presence and identity; consideration of the value and relevance of the mediums to academia; the opportunities and potential uses of the platforms with regard to self-promotion, networking and research activities; consideration of the value of writing and sharing less formally, but still academically, with a new audience; and the place of 'the social' in research life. Formal measurement of the fulfilment of these outcomes was not sought within this session, but it could be gauged to some degree through attendee comments and questions during the classes. However, there was a firm intention to build on the foundations laid in the sessions through practical follow-up and consultations beyond the classroom, take-up of which would point up whether our outcomes had been met.

Activities, resources and takeaways

The Twitter session involved an initial icebreaker activity designed to 'take the room's Twitter temperature' using a traffic light theme with green, amber and red post-it notes being selected by attendees to represent where they were with the platform: advocate (green); 'on the fence' (amber); confirmed sceptic and/or non-user (red). On the coloured post-its attendees were also invited to write the down the reason for their selection. This was a useful scene-setter, pointing up as it did the concerns and questions held by the audience. The blogging session perhaps suffered from the absence of a similar activity to gauge where users already were with that medium.

Aside from the Prezi, Twitter attendees were pointed to a range of resources, links and articles housed on our new media blog.[1] Blogging attendees were sent an e-mail after the session linking to a summary blogpost of the event with links to all the blogs that were featured as well as some 'Getting Started' links for WordPress and Blogger. In both cases the support and knowledge of the information and library team was also flagged up as an ongoing resource.

Although there was no formal reflective component to either session, attendees were encouraged to consider if the session had 'opened their eyes' and/or brought them to a new understanding of either platform (in the case of Twitter, whether they would select a different coloured post-it note by the end of the session). Nevertheless, the content of each session was reflective in tone by design, with regular questions relating to voice, perceived risks of use, and to what extent personal and professional boundaries should be blurred.

Feedback was gathered via slips with smileys on which attendees could record their session experience in respect of duration, presenters and content. There was also space for them to respond to the media presented and to indicate whether they had been 'converted' or were at least now willing to give them a go. Of course, the follow-up sessions requested afterwards also stand as a form of positive feedback.

Personal reflection

Both sessions emphasized the need for increased instruction and advice in this growing area. There is a definite opportunity here for library and information workers to demonstrate that awareness of online identity, social media opportunities (and threats) and choice of communication channels should now be an important component of everyone's information skill-set and that we are ideally placed to offer such advice and support. It also struck me that this area is highly personal and that any teaching must recognize this and be inherently accepting of the fact that attendee viewpoints will differ wildly, dependent on learner experiences and preferred approaches. Leading these sessions demonstrated to me that this strand of ANCIL is a very important element of our teaching programme and has much in common with all the others, given that it guides the user to evaluate and reflect on information choices, tools and platforms.

Pedagogical principles

The sessions and the ANCIL approach also led me to reflect on the pedagogical principles that generally guide me in my teaching. My experiences of teaching and being taught, and my grateful and ready adoption of ideas from my peers in the profession, have led to a veritable ragbag of ideas and techniques informing my approaches. I say 'approaches' because I have found that, above all, every session I teach or facilitate must be highly tailored and contextually appropriate to the students attending it. In my early years as a less confident librarian I led enough non-specific inductions and lectures to know that a generic approach – with the same lecture being delivered to different groups of students – makes for a negative experience all round: if the students to whom I was presenting were not engaged, then I was not engaged, and if I was not engaged . . . a vicious circle.

Although I have not always necessarily realized it, I have largely adopted a constructivist approach to teaching: essentially the idea that learners construct knowledge and meaning for themselves as they learn. I am not unusual in believing that learning should be an active process for learners as they engage with knowledge, testing and exploring it rather than passively accepting it. In the evaluation of information quality, value and presentation, we librarians have a prime topic ready and waiting for active learners to grapple with, so there is really no excuse for any of us settling for passively delivered and received teaching sessions. Occasionally a lack of time, rather than laziness, has led me to cut a few corners and, as a result, engage less than I otherwise might. But just like the scolded pupil I know that when I take this route I've only been cheating myself! I have come to realize that in order for learners to have more of an opportunity to be active in my classes I have needed to assume the role of a facilitator, or conversation-starter, rather than a didactic teacher, with a view to learners more easily reaching their own understanding of the content.

I'm very aware that my own preferred personal styles have also inevitably informed my pedagogical choices. Under Honey and Mumford's (1992) learning styles definitions I have a strong preference for an 'Activist' approach: I learn by doing and feel the need to dive right in, while under Kolb's (1984) experiential learning styles I am an 'Accommodator', leaning strongly towards concrete experience and active experimentation. As such, I have had a tendency to neglect more reflective and observational components, something that a template like ANCIL can usefully remind me to include. Kolb recognized that experiential learning was a cycle and I think my teaching choices have not always taken my students on a circular enough trip and therefore the learning taking place has not perhaps been as effective or complete as it could have been.

For most of my working life I have been teaching postgraduates, many of whom have already had experience of working in the commercial sector after their first degree, with the average age of an MBA student at both Cambridge and Oxford being around 28. As this is the case I have found myself drawn to an approach that recognizes that adults have different learning leads from adolescents or children, in other words *andragogy* (from the Greek: 'man-leading') rather than pedagogy ('child-leading'). Knowles (2011) outlines an andragogical model which I have found particularly useful and applicable. His model recognizes, among a total of six assumptions, that adults: 'need to know why they need to learn something before undertaking to learn it'; 'develop a deep psychological need to be seen by others and treated by others as capable of self-direction'; and 'will be more heterogeneous in terms of background, learning style, motivation, needs, interests, and goals than is true of a group of youths', making individualization of teaching strategies very important (Knowles, 2011, 63–7).

I find Knowles's assumptions realistic and insightful and moreover complementary to a desire to facilitate with a view to engendering active learners rather than didactically teaching to passive learners. Having said that, I have also fronted the occasional lecture to undergraduates following a more andragogical approach and have come unstuck: faced with a sea of blank and frightened faces, I saw it dawn on them that I wanted them to talk to me and tell me what they think, not the other way around, and the silence was deafening. This brings me back to the point that I need to construct each teaching session to be tailored and contextually appropriate.

Even among management students of the same age, different courses and classes have a different feel and expectation of you as a teacher or facilitator. Without wishing to generalize too much, finance students are in the main going to want the facts, and quickly, and aren't necessarily going to appreciate humorous asides and anecdotes, while MBAs, again in general, are more happy for you to lead them round the houses before getting to the point, provided you are entertaining *and* genuinely funny. And yet these groups are themselves made up of a hugely diverse and international collection of students and what might work for the majority, in terms of witty asides and relevant stories, might be lost on others. I have found that I have to think less locally and more globally to get the references, and therefore the connection, right. And connection is – of course – the key, as it's this that needs to be created and maintained as we teach with a view to effective learning taking place.

Note

1   http://newmediaforresearchers.wordpress.com.

Bibliography

Honey, P. and Mumford, A. (1992) *The Manual of Learning Styles*, 3rd edn, Peter Honey Publications.

Knowles, M. (2011) *The Adult Learner: the definitive classic in adult education and human resource development,* 7th edn, Butterworth-Heinemann.

Kolb, D. A. (1984) *Experiential Learning: experience as the source of learning and development,* Prentice-Hall.

Priestner, A. (2011) The Value of Blogging, *Libreaction,* 9 December, http://libreaction.wordpress.com/2011/12/09/the-value-of-blogging.

Priestner, A. (2012a) A Review of Twitter for Research, *Libreaction,* 27 February, http://libreaction.wordpress.com/2012/02/27/a-review-of-twitter-for-research.

Priestner, A. (2012b) *Twitter for Research* [Prezi], http://prezi.com/eb9huuoeikcp/twitter-for-research.

Strand Nine

Synthesizing information and creating new knowledge

Emma Coonan

Strand Nine covers the higher-order intellectual operations around information, and again falls outside more traditional models of information literacy. The strand includes formulating research questions and learning to frame problems. This will include using chosen information sources to articulate and analyse problems in your discipline. It also incorporates assimilating information within the disciplinary framework, weighing the value of new information, and developing new insights and knowledge.

In many disciplines demonstrating these abilities may not be required or assessed until third-year or even postgraduate level, when students conduct an extended piece of work such as a dissertation. In these contexts the transition to conducting independent research may entail a significant step up in expectations and performance, and should be supported accordingly. In other disciplines (particularly arts or humanities subjects), evaluation, synthesis, voice and register are foregrounded almost from the beginning. In all cases, the development of these complex information-handling operations must be scaffolded as an integral part of academic learning.

Emma was the obvious choice to write the ninth case study in this book, given her role in developing ANCIL, but also her experience at Cambridge in leading and delivering the Research Skills Programme. While this case study focuses on Strand Nine, there are several other themes woven into the session that Emma teaches, which develops students' academic writing and reading and helps them learn about the academic practices of their discipline and how to synthesize and create new knowledge. The element of reflection is particularly strong in this case study.

Institutional context

The Research Skills Programme at Cambridge University Library offers specialist provision in various aspects of information literacy, including information and data management, finding and evaluating literature, academic writing and critical thinking. Its Information Skills strand provides eight sessions, which are aligned with either key academic practices such as literature searching and referencing, or specific phases in the study and research processes, including dissertation research at both undergraduate and Masters level. While each session is free-standing, the programme is designed to fit together in a modular, scaffolded fashion, so that participants can build their information-handling abilities and insight over the course of their subject career.

Each session is available as a bespoke course for subject cohorts, but take-up has been modest and is therefore far from comprehensive. As a result, the majority of Research Skills sessions are open classes available to participants from all subject disciplines, as well as to non-members of the university who use the library for private research and to visiting members of other institutions. The programme's focus is therefore necessarily on the development of common academic information practices that span the disciplines. To counteract the 'one-shot', standalone nature of this provision there is a strong emphasis on reflection and active participation.

A key principle underlying all session content is to go beyond simply offering skills training, instead aiming to support the whole academic process, including the development of scholarly attitudes and behaviours. As a result, sessions do not revolve around a single tool, skill or resource, but reflect and support the broader range of practices and values involved in study and research. This principle reflects the ANCIL vision, which identifies information literacy as a complex entity: not a static competency set but a continuum embracing skills and abilities and also attitudes and values (Coonan, 2011; Coonan and Secker, 2011).

Session development and overview

This chapter will look in depth at 'Academic Reading and Writing', a two-hour, face-to-face workshop designed as an introduction to the role and conventions of structure in academic writing. Originally designed in response to a faculty request for students on a part-time Masters course, it is now run four to six times a year in the Research Skills Programme. It attracts participants from a wide range of subject disciplines, chiefly postgraduates.

The session content aligns closely with ANCIL's Strand Nine, which includes the creative or transformative aspects of academic practice: assimilating and evaluating new information within the disciplinary framework, formulating questions and framing problems, and creating new knowledge. It is closely linked to and builds on the content of Strand Three, taking an academic literacies approach to reading and writing, as well as complementing the 'Presenting and Communicating Knowledge' focus of Strand Eight. However, the class focuses on two key aspects of reading and writing, which directly support the objectives of Strand Nine. First, it offers a reading strategy that enables students to assimilate and evaluate information efficiently and systematically, to expand their evolving conceptual map of their topic; second, it presents writing as a means to explore, question and synthesize previous contributions in the literature, and also to clarify and develop the researcher's own standpoint and vision.

It is hoped that the session content thus helps students to realize a reflective framework in which the academic practices of reading and writing with which they have engaged during their undergraduate career or the first part of the Masters course can now be used in the service of framing problems, articulating incisive research questions and synthesizing a range of viewpoints from existing knowledge to support the researcher's own contribution to the discipline.

Format and platform

The workshop is run in small-group or boardroom layout, with the entire class, including the session leader, seated around one or more tables. It is extremely (and deliberately) low-tech: the focus is on active engagement with reading and writing, and therefore the main materials are a scholarly article of each participant's choice and his or her preferred writing implements. Two double-sided handouts are distributed: 'How to read 10 books in an hour' and 'Essay writing survival guide' (both freely available to download and share[1]). No slides are used, although a flipchart or whiteboard is useful for noting points that arise from general discussion. The absence of slides, like the seating of the session leader among participants, is intended to break down the formal teacher–student relationship as far as possible and instead create an environment in which participants actively contribute to and shape the session, facilitating the emergence of the student as a specialist in his or her discipline. It also makes for an extremely flexible and 'portable' session, which can be run in a variety of environments.

Learning outcomes

'Academic Reading and Writing' directly addresses two areas of the research process that are of paramount concern to students: staying on top of the volume of reading expected of them, and writing in what is seen to be the 'approved' academic manner. Like other Research Skills sessions, the class also has a demystificatory function, aiming to help students 'break the code' of academic expectations.

It is hoped that by the end of the session participants will be able to:

- use strategic reading techniques to sift, evaluate and assimilate material quickly and efficiently
- recognize and deploy structural conventions appropriate to their discipline
- manage the processes of essay planning and writing, including free writing early in the process
- use appropriate techniques to break through writer's block.

The session content also aligns with ANCIL's four learning bands (see page xxv). The practical skills taught are skim-reading and active note-making; the subject context is brought by the student, and lies in the ability to recognize and articulate the structural conventions that characterize scholarly writing generally, and the specific expressions of these conventions peculiar to each participant's discipline. The concepts of research as a dialogue and of writing as thinking help to reframe writing as an ongoing exploration rather than a final commitment, facilitating synthesis and problem framing. This forms the advanced information-handling element. Finally, re-conceiving the relationship between reading and writing as interrelated components of the thinking process enables participants to develop a flexible, evolving and reflective approach to their performance that transcends the academic context and contributes to lifelong learning.

Reading strategies
Strategic reading techniques

The first half of the class focuses on strategic reading techniques designed to enable quick and efficient assimilation of scholarly texts. In this section the participant as reader is the primary audience, and the work's structure is discussed as a means of identifying key navigation points for skim-reading. The function and scope of various parts of the work, including abstract, introduction and conclusion, are discussed in general terms, and section headings, figures and the first sentences of paragraphs are explored as a means of pinpointing the argumentative 'skeleton' or outline of the work.

Once the reader feels confident that the main argument of the work has been grasped by means of navigating through the key structural elements, the technique of quick scanning is introduced to enable participants to engage with selected short sections of the work that they feel merit or require fuller attention. Scanning is also a 'quick' reading strategy, explained as being akin to flicking through a newspaper rather than the close, linear reading we might perform on (for example) a work of fiction. The key take-home message is: when you feel you have got enough out of the text, stop reading.

Discussion in sessions indicates that many participants feel at first that reading the whole text sequentially is 'better' (more virtuous) than skimming; yet participants also recognize that reading continuously and sequentially can induce passivity and loss of concentration, as well as a loss of focus on the research question. This dilemma echoes the conflict between virtue and effectiveness in study practices articulated by Cottrell (2008, 64), which makes an extremely useful discussion point in class.

Continuous reading also risks undermining critical objectivity, as readers may be swayed by rhetoric rather than evidence. Strategic skimming and scanning of key structural elements of the work, on the other hand, allows students to both save time and maintain critical distance. It provides them with a tool that enables them not only to assimilate new material in their discipline effectively, but also to assess its relationship to their own research question and evaluate how it informs their emerging view of the research topic.

Strategic reading can also deepen students' recognition and understanding of how scholarly writing is practised in their own discipline. It offers them a framework through which to compare how different writers on the same topic present and structure their arguments, how they handle supporting and conflicting evidence, and how they counterpoint their own voice and viewpoint with those of the authors whom they cite. Consciously examining how published authors manage these aspects of scholarly writing enables students to compare, evaluate and if desired emulate approaches that they find successful.

Participants are given five minutes in which to practise skim-reading the article which they have brought to class. They are then asked to reflect on and discuss how useful they found the approach as a means of both efficiently absorbing key content and critically evaluating work in their topic. They are also asked to consider how successful they were at resisting the temptation to read continuously, and therefore risk being drawn into the author's argument. Pickard's metaphor of the 'white rabbit' (2007, 56) – a theme or pathway that leads away from the research question and causes the researcher to lose focus – is described here to highlight the importance of maintaining critical distance from the text and a clear vision of the researcher's own approach and question.

The 'student as specialist' activity

After the initial strategic reading exercise using an article of their own choice, participants are asked to swap articles with a neighbour from a different subject domain and perform the exercise again. This activity is designed to bring out participants' latent awareness of how voice, register and structure function in the writing of their discipline. They are asked to identify and discuss aspects of the writing that strike them as noticeably 'different' or alien, and suggest what intervention would be necessary to align the work more closely with their own discipline. Participants thus begin to consciously recognize and articulate not only the characteristics of general scholarly writing but also disciplinary differences, enabling them to choose how to deploy the compositional conventions predominant in their own subject to best effect.

The article-swapping exercise creates an opportunity for class participants to express latent or part-realized awareness of how academic writing is performed in their own field. Since the session leader is – necessarily! – not a specialist in the discourse of each subject, it is entirely up to participants to articulate how structure, tenor and language differ from article to article, and to decide how far this extends into differences between disciplines. Each class thus builds upon participants' contributions as they explore and begin to articulate the conventions implicitly at play not only in the framework and discourse of their field but also in how they perform their own research practices.

The concept of the student as specialist is informed by Hepworth and Walton's (2009) view of information literacy as embodied in an individual performing a specific task within a given context at a particular time in his or her development. What each learner brings to the class is at least as important as what the session leader contributes, and in the context of academic writing, which can only be performed by the individual operating within a given subject context, it is the participants who must make the connections between the practice they have encountered in their discipline and their own ongoing development as academic writers.

Writing, thinking and synthesis

By this point in the class, participants' verbal feedback generally indicates that they have already started to consider the role of structure in their own compositional writing. Here the concept of writing as thinking is introduced, and a distinction drawn between the linear, sequential construction of the finished work, which corresponds to the key strategic navigation points discussed in the first part of the class, and the early, messier, exploratory writing that evolves over several drafts to that finished piece. The session thus aims to unpack the complex role of scholarly writing and look at both the construction and characteristics of the final, polished, 'academic' entity, and the creative role of writing as a means of sparking both insight and synthesis as the student moves towards producing that final entity.

The role of writing in clarifying, synthesizing and expanding one's own thought is often new to participants, who have frequently been led to consider thinking, reading and writing as discrete steps in the process of performing research. The session aims to combat this tendency to defer the writing phase, first by discussing these issues and asking students to share their experiences of (and anxieties around) writing. We then look at the concept of reading, thinking and writing as a dynamic, integrated and iterative practice that is fundamental to the development of a research topic, instead of separate, sequential and qualitatively different steps in the research process.

The metaphor of research as a dialogue (most famously depicted by Burke, 1975, 94–6) is useful here. Interrogating and 'answering back' to the literature releases researchers from the passive role of merely assimilating knowledge and licenses them to take an active part in the conversation. This is a good point at which to raise the powerful potential of note-making as an active process linking reading and writing. 'Double entry' note-making, for example, encourages the reader simultaneously to record useful source material and reflect on how and where it fits into the researcher's own conceptual landscape of the topic. This deepens familiarity with the existing context and at the same time places the researcher in a position to start probing the topic and formulating research questions; it also establishes the habit of writing as an ongoing, exploratory engagement with the topic from an early stage.

Writing strategies discussed in the session include mapping out themes; starting in the middle rather than with the introduction; generating 'chunked' writing that can be juxtaposed and joined together later; and above all, free, exploratory, 'messy' writing to capture the thought process. Techniques for maintaining the habit of writing every day, such as setting a specific time period or word limit, are also explored. Writing is presented as a thinking tool, an exploratory process that assists the researcher 'to experiment, to revise, to repeat and to reconceptualize' (Murray and Moore, 2006, 5). Thus writing becomes not the final step in a linear process but an iterative engagement with the topic that aids emergence and development of the researcher's thought and the creation of insight, 'a vital tool in discovery and learning' (Ballenger, 2012, xxv).

To enable students to actively engage and experiment with this concept, the session finishes with a free-writing exercise in which participants are asked to write for five minutes, without stopping, spellchecking or editing.

Pedagogic principles

The generic approach enforced by the open, 'one-shot' nature of the Research Skills Programme is often – and rightly – perceived as a weakness in information literacy teaching (Wingate, 2006; see also Whitworth, 2006). However, teaching groups of participants from a range of disciplines has one major benefit: it can help to uncover the behaviours, expectations and values of the academic community, which are frequently left unexplained, and indeed unarticulated, on the bland assumption that the student will pick them up by accident or osmosis (Weetman, 2005; Badke, 2010). Classes with participants from a mix of subjects can benefit from opportunities to discuss and compare the academic practice they have encountered. Much of the content of the Research Skills Programme therefore has a demystificatory aspect in which unspoken practices are brought to light and explored, and the programme is founded on a vision of the student not as a passive receiver of knowledge but as an active participant in its creation.

In my classes I position myself as someone with experience of various academic contexts, rather than an expert. Where I can illustrate my teaching with an example from my own experience as an undergraduate, Masters student, doctoral student or researcher, I will do so, as I find that participants respond well to 'real-life' examples of information-handling activity and their implications for academic success or failure. However, this sharing of experience is also intended to encourage participants to describe their own tools, techniques and approaches. This creates a culture of peer sharing and support in classes, giving me as well as participants many useful new tips and strategies; but also helps participants to reflect on 'how they do what they do'. As Beetham, McGill and Littlejohn point out, 'in higher education, learning is about being able to take up a personal stance in relation to subject knowledge and expertise' (2009, 70) and it is this ability to take up a stance, to offer an informed and individual perspective, that I try to foster in all my sessions.

Academic writing is the concrete embodiment of taking up a personal stance. However, this practice seems to suffer most from the failure to articulate clearly what is expected of the student. As Lillis (2001, x) points out, all too often we demand that students 'write within the rules of the game without knowing what the rules [are]'. Academic writing is a deceptively complex practice, requiring an understanding of 'the ways with words that the institution values' and the ability to deploy the 'appropriate linguistic capital' (Lillis (2001, x).

In addition, in the early stages of a research project the desire to acquire a reliable body of subject knowledge and a firm grasp of the topic often leads students into an immersive phase of reading, with a concomitant reluctance – that may harden into obstinacy – towards committing themselves in writing to a standpoint that could later prove flawed. The demand to make an original contribution to knowledge is often literally inconceivable at first: how is the researcher to postulate an end-point to the project when that project has only just begun? How to come up with a good research question before being familiar with the whole field? What if the research has already been done?

The anxiety induced by this position can be crippling, and often results in 'one more article syndrome' (Beals, 2012), in which researchers focus on simply assimilating more and more literature on the topic without responding to it or reflecting on how it informs their own perspective and argument.

Through its practical approaches to reading and writing and the opportunity to discuss and compare how these practices are performed in various disciplines, the session described here aims to help students position themselves as actively involved in the academic dialogue and therefore in creating meaning. A variety of tools and approaches to help them achieve these aims are explored:

1   The practical skills of skim-reading and active note-making give participants essential strategies for assimilating information in their field.
2   Developing the concept of 'answering back' to the dialogue releases researchers from the passive role of merely assimilating knowledge and licenses them to take an active part in the conversation.
3   The idea of the 'student as specialist', which informs the article-swap activity and discussion, builds on this by asking students to draw out and articulate what they have already experienced of academic practice in their discipline, then compare it with others' experience.
4   The concept and practice of writing-as-thinking, incorporated from an early stage, supports the development of the researcher's own voice and emerging standpoint by ensuring that literature is not only recorded but interrogated, responded to, synthesized and reflected upon in the light of the researcher's own perspective.

I hope that this case study illustrates that cross-disciplinary provision need not be purely skills-focused, bolt-on or remedial. As shown above, classes involving participants from a mix of disciplines can facilitate the articulation of hidden conventions and expectations by drawing on each participant's own experience of scholarly practices. The opportunity to discuss and compare how these often unarticulated academic practices operate in different subject groups can in turn help to uncover and demystify the behaviours, expectations and values of the wider academic community.

'Academic Reading and Writing' aims to make the demands of the learning culture more transparent and by doing so to empower individual learners to take control of and responsibility for their own learning experience. When students are invited to make connections between information-handling practices and values and their own engagement in the processes of study and research, it is possible to create an environment in which learners have the opportunity to bring their own practices to the table and reflect on them; to consider what is expected of them at each stage of their academic career; and to develop a learning framework that enables them to make informed choices about how they operate in the academic environment – and succeed in it.

Note

1   http://researchcentral.wordpress.com/academic-reading-and-writing.

Bibliography

Badke, W. (2010) Why Information Literacy is Invisible, *Communications in Information Literacy*, **4** (2), 129–41.

Ballenger, B. (2012) *The Curious Researcher: a guide to writing research papers*, Longman Press.

Beals, M. H. (2012) Like Water for Horses; or, why even good students don't do multiple drafts, http://melodeebeals.co.uk/like-water-for-horses-or-why-even-good-students-dont-do-multiple-drafts/.

Beetham, H., McGill, L. and Littlejohn, A. (2009) *Thriving in the 21st Century: learning literacies for the digital age*, www.jisc.ac.uk/media/documents/projects/llidareportjune2009.pdf.

Bent, M. (2008) *Perceptions of Information Literacy in the Transition to Higher Education*, http://eprint.ncl.ac.uk/pub_details2.aspx?pub_id=55850#.

Burke, K. (1975) *The Philosophy of Literary Form: studies in symbolic action,* Vintage Press.

Coonan, E. (2011) *Teaching Learning: perceptions of information literacy*, http://newcurriculum.wordpress.com/project-reports-and-outputs/.

Coonan, E. and Secker, J. (2011) *A New Curriculum for Information Literacy: curriculum and supporting documents*, http://newcurriculum.wordpress.com/project-reports-and-outputs/.

Cottrell, S. (2008) *The Study Skills Handbook*, 3rd edn, Palgrave Macmillan.

Hepworth, M. and Walton, G. (2009) *Teaching Information Literacy for Inquiry-Based Learning*, Chandos Press.

Lillis, T. (2001) *Student Writing: access, regulation, desire*, Routledge Press.

Murray, R. and Moore, S. (2006) *The Handbook of Academic Writing: a fresh approach*, Open University Press.

Pickard, A. (2007) *Research Methods in Information*, Facet Publishing.

Weetman, J. (2005) Osmosis: does it work for the development of information literacy?, *Journal of Academic Librarianship*, **31** (5), 456–60 .

Whitworth, A. (2006) Communicative Competence in the Information Age: towards a critical theory of information literacy education, *Italics*, **5** (1), www.ics.heacademy.ac.uk/italics/vol5iss1.htm.

Wingate, U. (2006) Doing Away with Study Skills, *Teaching in Higher Education*, **11** (4), 457–69.

Strand Ten

The social dimension of information

Helen Webster

Strand Ten is perhaps the most transformational of all the strands as the learner evolves into a lifelong learner, developing a critical awareness of how their learning will continue beyond formal education. The strand supports the development of strategies for assimilating new information as well as information-handling, problem-solving and decision-making skills for the workplace and for the choices of daily life. Strand Ten also includes an understanding of the ethics and politics of information, so the learner develops strategies for assimilating and analysing information that might challenge their world view.

We first met Helen through her work on the Transkills project at the University of Cambridge,[1] which seeks to facilitate the transition of first-year undergraduates from their prior learning experiences to study at university. It quickly became clear that there were many parallels between our work and Helen's project, and her background as a learning developer also led to many fascinating conversations. Transition is an important theme throughout ANCIL, appearing not only in Strand One (Transition into higher education) but perhaps more importantly in this final strand, as the transition out of the academic environment into lifelong learning. Helen's experience as an academic and learning developer, as well as her subsequent Arcadia research from October to December 2012 to explore strategies for implementing ANCIL, make this case study to explore the final tenth strand particularly welcome.

Background and institutional context

As a new profession, learning development draws on and complements various other professions which offer teaching, coaching, guidance and advice on information literacy, from subject lecturing, counselling, careers and disability support, to librarianship (see Hilsdon, 2011, 13–27). Those working in learning development may be located in various institutional contexts under different job titles, and bring with them a variety of professional backgrounds and theoretical frameworks (Murray and Glass, 2011). Some are located in Student Services, others in libraries, others in faculties and departments, and all work closely with colleagues from these sectors across an institution. Much of my work as a learning developer has taken the form of one-to-one sessions, experience which has been invaluable in informing my workshop provision and resource development with a learner-centred perspective. When first starting out in this type of work, I drew on my teacher training, which offered theoretical frameworks of learning, but, being geared more to the classroom, little in the way of practical models around which to structure my one-to-one sessions. I looked instead to models from counselling, careers guidance and also the reference interview from the field of librarianship. I found in ANCIL a model which complemented and drew these together into an approach more focused on the type of work performed by learning developers in higher education, while promoting an interprofessional awareness of the complexity of a student's learning.

Much study support provision within higher education is primarily concerned with facilitating students in successful induction and integration into the practices and cultures of academia. Social aspects of information literacy, while alluded to as 'lifelong learning' in course documentation and prospectuses, are often equated with employability, and rarely genuinely embedded into the curriculum, as both students and subject lecturers are more focused on the subject learning and assessment task immediately to hand. Learning developers, who have limited time with a student and little agency in the timing of these interactions, may be equally focused on the specific and immediate issue the students have brought to them. One of the recurring and most important challenges for learning developers, and indeed other higher education professionals, is to encourage the student to see past this particular essay or exam to wider reflection on learning and the development of strategies which they can bring to bear no matter what the assignment. To promote lifelong learning in addition to this can sometimes seem a challenge too far, and is easily relegated to the remit of another profession – the subject lecturers or the Careers Service.

Strand Ten, of all the strands, is perhaps too remote in the student's mind and too low a priority in the midst of coursework and exams for them to engage with explicitly, and thus it must be truly embedded in every aspect of the course and associated provision. Helping students to develop as lifelong learners should be everyone's remit in higher education, as perhaps the most significant, longest-lasting benefit they will derive, long after the subject knowledge has been forgotten. And, as is so often the case, good provision in one instance is good provision in all; thinking about how to embed lifelong learning may well give rise to a consideration of how to embed other aspects of information literacy, so that the model of requesting 'bolt-on' provision from learning developers and librarians gives way to a consultative, collaborative and interprofessional approach to course design and teaching. Lifelong learning may also become a vehicle through which to help students engage with the more pressing task of understanding the unfamiliar academic forms of information literacy which they are encountering at university, by grounding it back in the context of their personal or professional lives.

During my work as a learning developer at the University of East Anglia (UEA), I worked extensively with a cohort of students for whom the challenge of developing the attitudes and strategies of the lifelong learner is particularly vivid: those enrolled on professional healthcare courses, such as nursing, midwifery and other allied health professions (see Parker and Freeth, 2009). The transition *out* of university into lifelong learning takes on a peculiarly prominent status for these students, as they are being explicitly prepared from the start to join a particular profession after graduation, and lecturers take an overt interest in students' future learning and professional development beyond the course (Parker and Freeth, 2009, 451).

More significantly, the nature of these courses, with their regular clinical placements, requires the learner to switch constantly between identities during the degree itself. Most of these identities will be new and perhaps at odds with the learner's sense of self, and with each other: parent or family member, student peer (with all the lifestyle expectations that this connotes), learner at a university, and competent professional on placement (Parker and Freeth, 2009, 450). These last two roles are somewhat in conflict with each other, with the student alternatively and in quick succession required to present themselves as a learner whose incomplete knowledge of the subject is assumed and accepted, and a junior healthcare professional who must instil confidence in their patients. They must engage not only with their own learning, but with that of others, both inside and outside their profession, preparing to become a mentor themselves for future students of their profession, understanding other professions in order to be able to work interprofessionally with them, and entering into an often sensitive dialogue with patients regarding their lay handling of health information (Parker and Freeth, 2009). The professional healthcare student is constantly transitioning between the academic context and 'the real world'. Where students on other courses may view lifelong learning as something which happens after they graduate, for professional healthcare students this constant switching between identities and between learning/professional contexts brings learning beyond formal education to the fore, and with it the need to develop appropriate strategies for assimilating new information from different contexts.

Academic literacies

Students often feel, and may be encouraged to feel, that the academic practices of critical thinking and information handling are unique to the academic context, alien and contrary to their wealth of experience in other areas of their lives. In higher education, information literacy tasks are formally and carefully designed, thus making information literacy itself visible as a goal and process, given additional value through assessment and feedback. In other spheres of life, an individual's information literacy may go undesigned, unaccredited, unremarked and thus unnoticed or unvalued. Students may feel that the various spheres of their lives, associated identities and information literacy practices must be kept rigidly separate from one another, that learning to handle information in the academic context is to 'rectify' the faulty thinking of social, domestic or 'real-life' work contexts.

If anything, the assumption is that the information literacy practices they learn in the academic sphere might 'enrich' other areas of their life, but that this interaction is one-way only. Lifelong learning is thus conceived in a linear, timeline fashion and positioned as a 'correction' of naive information literacy by academic values and practices, which either perfects the learner's thinking from graduation onwards, or deteriorates as the learner leaves their period in higher education further behind. Providing opportunities for students to reflect on their own conception of and assumptions about lifelong learning can help to address tensions between and reconcile their identities in various spheres of life, and promote a sense of ownership over the unfamiliar modes of academic thinking.

Exploring academic literacies is an approach to learning development which 'views student writing and learning as issues at the level of epistemology and identities rather than skill or socialisation' (Lea and Street, 1998, 159; see also pages 27–40 in this book). It explicitly acknowledges and values the other identities and ways of knowing that students bring to university learning and views the learning developer's task as one of clarifying the assumptions and expectations brought by lecturers and students to the task of learning, without necessarily privileging the academic as pre-eminent or negating other ways of knowing or being but encouraging the student to use the most appropriate approach to the task.

From the student's point of view, a dominant feature of academic literary practices is the requirement to switch practices between one setting and another, to deploy a repertoire of linguistic practices appropriate to each setting, and to handle the social meanings and identities that each evokes. This emphasis on identities and social meanings draws attention to deep affective and ideological conflicts in such switching and use of the linguistic repertoire (Lea and Street, 1998, 159).

The academic literacies approach was developed, and is usually applied, in the context of academic writing. However, the notion of different spheres in which the student assumes appropriate identities and practices is a very useful one in developing broader information literacy, both in supporting the studying during the transition to university and in thinking about the transition to lifelong learning in contexts beyond university study. I view lifelong learning not as a linear continuation of the academic mode of learning, but as this ability to adapt to new learning contexts by switching between identities and practices appropriate to them. The academic identity and practice of information literacy is to the fore, not necessarily because it is intrinsically better, but because university study offers students the opportunity and the means to reflect on their information literacy and learning, to articulate it and to have it acknowledged and assessed, so that they have a space in which to engage with it actively and thoughtfully. Not only would it be a waste if the opportunity to encourage students to reflect on other learning contexts were missed, but in not making the connection between the academic and other 'everyday' modes of learning, we may be making the process of learning the rather alien values and practices of academic learning more difficult to grasp.

Reflective exercises

From my work with professional healthcare students at UEA, I have built up a repertoire of reflective exercises which help students to conceptualize the unfamiliar information literacy values and practices they need to learn and apply in the academic context, by grounding them in cognate activities in other areas of their lives. Drawing on an academic literacies approach, I use the notion of spheres of life and the various identities that students develop and assume in response, and encourage students to consider how these identities might be equally valued and how they interplay and enrich each other in the process of lifelong learning, rather than superseding one another until learners feel they are being asked to become someone who they are not. I ask them to reflect on how they might draw on their existing information literacy approaches to address an academic problem which requires them to develop and apply unfamiliar information literacy values and practices, and vice versa. I use the term 'lens' to describe the different approaches they might bring from the different spheres of their lives to help them 'see' an information literacy task in various ways.

The exercises address a number of academic information literacy tasks which students initially find alien or unfamiliar, and which they may struggle to grasp when presented in academic terminology. These tasks might include the need to develop and articulate a 'conceptual or theoretical framework', to 'think critically', to 'synthesize the scholarship as a literature review' or discern the difference between the learning needed for a coursework assignment and an exam. All of these tasks, while seemingly new to the students and unique to the academic context, have cognate activities in other areas of their lives. The point at which these exercises might usefully be introduced will depend partly on the structure of the course, or on a particular student's reflection and engagement with feedback, if a student does not realize a need to develop his or her information literacy or puts off addressing it.

The work of a learning developer is varied and I find that I am able to adapt these exercises to fit the various forms of provision I offer, which range from one-to-one, student-initiated contexts to more formal teaching environments. Rather than comprising a whole session, therefore, this approach is flexible and designed to include an aspect of lifelong learning and transferable application to social learning contexts within workshops or tutorials on more specific academic activities. The exercises are strongly reflective in their nature, drawing on the students' personal lives external to their university identity, and thus I do not formally assess them. However, it is useful to get them to discuss their perspectives and reactions to their emerging academic identities and their relation to their identities in other spheres of life, to validate their approaches and articulate their conceptions of information literacy through discussion.

Rattus scholasticus

Strand Ten prompts the student to become a lifelong learner who can cope with the challenge of assimilating new information to their conceptual framework or world view. In the academic context, and particularly when working on dissertations, students are encouraged to develop or articulate a 'conceptual', 'theoretical' or 'critical' framework. These terms are very abstract, and many students find it difficult to grasp what it is that they are being asked to produce and what textual form it should take. The separation between the academic identity and the social, professional or domestic identities is very evident in students' difficulties with the conceptual framework. The conceptual framework seems something artificial which they 'make' especially for the dissertation, rather than something which emerges from the sum of their lived experience and informed reading, and which colours them and their outlook as a person in all facets of life.

If to be a lifelong learner is to develop strategies for assimilating new knowledge to your conceptual framework or to alter your world view in response to new learning, then the primary goal of the information literacy professional is to help students to render their own world view visible to themselves, articulate it and then to interrogate it. If the only context in which lifelong learners have been required to do this is at university, in response to a task which is quite new to them and for which they have had to construct a tailored conceptual framework out of materials which are also new to them, then it is unsurprising if they do not make the connection between this exercise and the almost unconscious set of values, beliefs and knowledge out of which they construct their response to the world every day.

In my one-to-one sessions and workshops, the question 'What does my supervisor mean when they tell me I have to define my conceptual framework?' is not uncommon in the context of dissertations. Of course, it is relevant for all types of academic work, not just those in which the delineation of the theoretical stance as a part of the text is a convention of the dissertation genre. I explain this issue by helping to make students' own world view more visible, and then moving on to examine how the academic 'conceptual framework' is a facet of this, and one which develops and changes. We then consider how the students' general world view has been constructed, and how it changes in response to new knowledge, either that gained in the context of their studies, or through other events in their lives.

To do this, I use an exercise which works in both workshop and individual sessions, although it is enhanced by having a range of conceptual frameworks from members of a group to contrast with their own and throw it into relief. I simply display an image of an object, as free from any leading contextual details as possible, which all of the students will have a strong reaction to or associations with. I like to use that of a rat, for reasons which I later explain to them. I ask them to write down the first word that comes into their head on seeing the image. We then share those words on a whiteboard or using post-it notes, and note the disparity of response between members of the group. Typical responses include 'vermin', 'dirty', 'plague', and on one occasion, 'politician'! If no one has yet offered it, I offer my own response: 'cute'. This usually results in some surprise – I explain that the image is one of my own pet fancy rats. In itself, it is a neutral object, but the different context in which I encounter this animal, and the experiences and knowledge which I have accrued inform my reaction to and concept of it (or rather, him!).

We discuss the reasons behind our responses, the 'knowledge', culture, values and experiences on which they are based, the context in which these were gained, and the way in which this image's place in our world view is shaped by them. We also look at evaluating the knowledge which informs our reaction, to question our own world view and contrast it with the different views of other group members, to show how it 'ain't necessarily so'. It is of course important to approach this exercise with non-judgemental sensitivity and intercultural awareness.

Next, I ask the students to think in terms of their own discipline: as healthcare professionals, or as history scholars, literature students, economists, biologists or sociologists. They are to write down a word that describes the image in the terms of their own subject. This time, the responses include words such as 'disease vector', 'laboratory model', 'metaphor or symbol', 'indicator of poverty', 'catalyst of social change', 'genus: *Rattus norvegicus*'. We discuss how this academic conceptual framework differs from their more general world view, and from each others', but also how each has developed out of their own information and experience as students. We examine how the academic framework has been more consciously and critically constructed, and differs according to discipline, but how the same might be true of the students' more general world view, which can be subjected to the same processes. We also consider how they each hold a number of such conceptual frameworks simultaneously, as different lenses through which they view an object, and how these perspectives might interact (contradictory or complementary) within a person's whole world view.

The three-year-old's guide to critical thinking

'Critical thinking' is another term which is frequently used at university with little concrete definition or strategies offered for performing it. It can seem one of the more frustrating barriers to healthcare students' learning goals – they are keen to acquire new knowledge, which they can apply successfully in the real world and in assignments, but the task of simultaneously questioning and undermining the value of the knowledge they are learning can seem perverse. Why recommend articles through reading lists or university library subscription if they're not reliable? Like 'conceptual framework', 'critical thinking' is only explicitly taught, assessed and articulated in the academic context, and this may seem to render their non-academic applications of it invisible, and possibly invalid.

For this exercise, I try to locate the practice of critical thinking in a non-academic context which students can easily recognize or relate to, because many of them are parents, aunts or uncles, and all of them have been children. I tell them that the sharpest critical thinker I know is my three-year-old niece, as she has an ability to ask very fundamental, penetrating and analytical questions. I encourage them to suggest from their own experience as parents, siblings or other familial relationships the questions that young children frequently ask. Responses typically include 'What's that?', 'How does that work?', 'What does that mean?', 'What's that for?', 'But why can't I? Daddy/Mummy said I could!' and the eternal 'Why?' Then I ask them to think about teenagers in their lives, including their former selves, and the questions that they typically ask. 'Why should I?', 'Says who?' and 'So what?' are often among the responses offered. We collate these questions into a list on the whiteboard, or using post-it notes.

The next step is to apply the questions to a piece of academic literature, to practise critical reading. I read aloud an article (from their reading list, or otherwise associated with their discipline or a current assignment if possible). Asking the students to channel their inner three- (or thirteen-) year-old self, I ask them to interrupt me at any time with an appropriate question from the list. Either the question is anticipated by the author of the article I'm reading and answered in the next sentence or two from the article, or a weakness or omission in the article is exposed which the students can build into their critical assessment of it. This might be done at some length with a group in which you are confident that all participants will be happy to shout out; generally I read a couple of paragraphs to illustrate the technique, and then switch to partner or small group work to ensure that they are all engaging actively. For groups who already have a good relationship, or as an individual exercise, this technique can also be applied to a piece of the student's own writing as a peer review exercise.

A further stage is to consider the typical answers to these questions. I ask the students what kind of answers are commonly given to children in response to their questions. Typical responses include 'Because I said so!', 'It just does', 'Ask your father' and answers that gloss over the real issue: 'The sky is blue because it's painted that colour'. We consider why these answers might (or might not!) be appropriate in the context of children, and what they are based on – appeals to authority, circular or other fallacious reasoning, impressive but meaningless statements. We consider what effective answers in the academic context might be based on, and why. We also consider whether there is ever a point in academic reasoning where you just have to stop pursuing a question and accept an answer as enough. Finally, I get students to return to the objections they identified in the academic article and offer suggestions of how the criticisms might have been answered by the author.

To bring the technique back to lifelong learning, we might then apply it to a non-academic text on a similar theme. The School of Nursing and Midwifery at UEA sets its midwives an assignment which does this very effectively. It gives students an article not from an academic journal but from a popular magazine about pregnancy and childcare, aimed at new mums, and asks them to not only write a critique of the information and give a fuller explanation of the scientific details which are missing from the lay article, but also consider why the article has been written as it has for a lay audience, and the appropriateness of the level at which the information has been aimed in this context. This assignment asks students to consider whether academic critical thinking is actually appropriate in contexts in which they will be working with a non-academic client, and to think about more appropriate ways of critiquing and offering information. Such an activity works very well as a workshop exercise, and in other disciplines, perhaps using a newspaper article or blog post.

Conclusion

These and similar exercises I use in my practice are designed to help explain and ground seemingly abstract, abstruse academic activities in everyday experience, in which cognate information literacy activities are performed by different 'identities', and to help students articulate and negotiate the interplay of these various 'lenses'. Whether working in a one-to-one tutorial or in a workshop, I find that students respond well to the suggestion that they have already developed a version of these skills in other areas of life, and to my valuing of their non-academic experience, as well as to the thoughtful re-examining of their everyday information literacy strategies.

Lifelong learning has long privileged academic modes of information literacy, and positioned the experience of academic learning as the pinnacle of a very linear approach to 'lifelong', but helping students to identify, develop and appropriately apply the different identities and practices proper to different spheres of life seems to me to be a better way to promote genuinely student-centred learning throughout their lives.

Note

1   http://skills.caret.cam.ac.uk/transkills.

Bibliography

Coonan, E. and Secker, J. (2011) *A New Curriculum for Information Literacy: curriculum and supporting documents*, http://newcurriculum.wordpress.com/project-reports-and-outputs/.

Hilsdon, J. (2011) What is Learning Development? In Hartley, P., Hilsdon, J., Keenan, C., Sinfield, S. and Verity, M. (eds), *Learning Development in Higher Education*, Palgrave Macmillan.

Lea, M. R. and Street, B. V. (1998) Student Writing in Higher Education: an academic literacies approach, *Studies in Higher Education*, **23** (2), 157–72.

Murray, L. and Glass, B. (2011) Learning Development in Higher Education: community of practice or profession? In Hartley, P., Hilsdon, J., Keenan, C., Sinfield, S. and Verity, M. (eds), *Learning Development in Higher Education*, Palgrave Macmillan.

Parker, P. and Freeth, D. (2009) Key Aspects of Teaching and Learning in Nursing and Midwifery. In Fry, H., Ketteridge, S. and Marshall, S. (eds), *A Handbook for Teaching and Learning in Higher Education: enhancing academic practice,* 3rd edn, Routledge.

Afterword

'Ownership is a flawed concept'

Katy Wrathall

Implementing the curriculum was the natural next phase after the creation and publication of ANCIL. The subsequent Arcadia Programme project, Strategies for Implementing ANCIL,[1] had two separate but complementary strands, one a 12-week project examining methods of implementing ANCIL within the University of Cambridge, and the other a 10-week project investigating strategies within non-Cambridge higher education institutions (HEIs). The focus of this latter investigation of potential strategies within non-Cambridge HEIs was to identify existing provision of information literacy teaching and find out which members of staff are involved in the delivery.

Information literacy has long been believed to be primarily the domain of academic librarians. In 1999 the SCONUL Information Skills Taskforce echoed Biddiscombe's (1999) assertion that 'There are few academic library services that do not now regard the teaching of information skills as an important part of their mission', arguing that:

> This is evident from recent trends of activity in this area of work, identified from data supplied by the Library and Information Statistics Unit at Loughborough University. The average number of hours spent by library staff providing orientation and post-orientation for students in SCONUL institutions has increased over the last six years from 13 hours to 22 (per 100 full time equivalent students).
>
> SCONUL (1999, 7)

The SCONUL research revealed some variations, and showed that in new universities library staff spent more time teaching – increasing over the previous six years 1993–1999 from 22 to 28 hours – whereas the research-led universities tended to spend less time on teaching (the figures were 6 to 17 hours). The report concluded that, despite the variation in time spent, the trend was clearly increasing overall: the 'number of users receiving orientation or post-orientation sessions is increasing overall from 36% to 46%, while appearing to be constant in the "new" universities at 60%' (SCONUL, 1999, 7).

Information literacy teaching has developed considerably since SCONUL first launched its Seven Pillars of Information Literacy. There is also a growing understanding that:

> Librarians alone can not provide an effective information literacy program for the entire student body on campus. When departmental faculty and librarians share the responsibility for the information literacy program, it can be implemented with a more coherent and systematic approach throughout the campus . . . .
>
> Information literacy therefore depends on collaboration among classroom faculty, academic administrators, librarians and other information professionals. In order to effectively implement a program all parties must be involved.
>
> Piloiu (2011)

Not only is information literacy being seen as a shared endeavour between academics, librarians, administrators and other learning support staff, there is a growing recognition that the way it is taught needs to change to be less didactic and more in line with a constructivist pedagogy.

Information literacy is closely associated with problem-, inquiry- or resource-based learning. It also needs to take advantage of good practice in the effective use of instructional pedagogies and technologies (Piloiu, 2011). As Farkas (2012) asserts: 'The librarian should become a facilitator; not telling students what it's important for them to know, but creating an environment in which students can learn and have their ideas challenged.' Finally, information literacy needs to be integrated into the disciplines' learning outcomes in a way that is clear and explicit to learners and teachers (Piloiu, 2011).

It is not clear to what extent such collaboration may exist, and it was therefore decided that ANCIL should form the basis of an audit of information literacy provision within two HEIs. This would provide information on existing provision across the institutions, whether this was formalized, and at what stage in an undergraduate's career it was delivered.

Project background

Due to the time constraints of the project only two HEIs could be audited. The first choice was University of Worcester, where Sarah Oxford, the Academic Liaison Librarian, had undertaken research into the effectiveness of information literacy within the institution (Oxford, 2011). Sarah works closely with a course leader in one of the faculties she supports to embed the teaching into course content and measure the effects of such teaching. It was believed that this work and the existing professional connections with the university would make it a good subject for one of the pilots.

Helen Westmancoat, Clare McCluskey and Debbi Boden kindly agreed to support the second pilot of the audit at York St John University. Clare McCluskey, the Academic Support Librarian, has done much work on creating information literacy partnerships in higher education (McCluskey, 2011). This pre-existing commitment to collaboration in information literacy provision made York St John University a logical choice for the second pilot.

Various levels of organization charts for both institutions were used to map the skills and support provision for formal, student-led, academic-led and embedded delivery. This enabled identification of areas where there was a potential overlap of provision and areas susceptible to a lack of provision, identification of those positioned and skilled to deliver the provision, and whether parity of provision exists.

The ten strands of ANCIL were used to form the basis of an Information Literacy Provision Audit Questionnaire (see Appendix 4). The aim was to create a map of the existing provision across an institution. The ANCIL strands were then further expanded into more specific questions such as 'Do you help students find their academic voice?', 'Do you help students evaluate new information?' and 'Do you help students understand how they are influenced?'. This was intended to ascertain whether respondents understood what was involved in each of the strands, whether they were involved in delivering them in full or in part, and whether delivery was formal and mandatory or informal and elective.

Respondents were asked to identify at what stages of the undergraduate timeline they support and help students (including teaching) and to identify those with whom they worked collaboratively on a formal basis. Further questions were asked as to 'ownership' or responsibility for information literacy, how to deliver the curriculum, any issues, which areas of an institution might be reluctant to change how provision was delivered, which areas would be 'champions' and who were the top influencers.

In order to test the effectiveness of the questions it was decided the survey would be carried out in different ways at University of Worcester and York St John University. At Worcester, in close collaboration with Sarah Oxford and Ellen Williams (Student Achievement Officer), individuals and teams were identified to take part in a series of one-to-one interviews. It was decided that the full set of questions would be asked of each interviewee to try to identify issues arising in different areas and professions.

At York St John the survey was distributed electronically, using the free version of SurveyMonkey. To encourage responses a shorter, more fact-finding version was used for those not involved in library and information work, while the latter group received the full version. Unfortunately the constraints imposed by SurveyMonkey meant that the longer survey had to be split into two, which may have had some adverse impact on responses.

Responses

In all, 37 responses were received across the two HEIs. Those who took part either as interviewees or by returning the survey held a variety of roles, which included:

- academic support librarians
- front-line librarians
- technical roles within library and information services (LIS)
- student services officers
- careers officers
- heads of service
- deputy deans
- heads of programmes and courses
- lecturers
- administrators.

This wide range of roles enabled a broad view of information literacy provision to be obtained.

Representatives of seven departments at University of Worcester participated in the face-to-face interviews. These were kept deliberately informal and scheduled to last between one and one and a half hours. As the project had no official base in the university, and in order to keep the location as neutral and informal as possible, the interviews were held in one of the coffee shops on site. The questionnaire was used as a script, and interviewees were asked to identify whether the support they provided was formal or informal, mandatory or voluntary and in conjunction with other areas or not.

It became evident that while interviewees often did not initially recognize their provision as falling within the ten ANCIL strands, they did so once the strands were expanded into the more specific questions. The questions appeared to provide an opportunity for reflection on their own practice for many of the participants, providing a greater insight into the structure of delivery and the occasional lack of awareness of the work in this field of other departments. All participants expressed keenness to work collaboratively and believed an interdisciplinary approach to be the ideal pattern, but they were all very aware of possible barriers to this.

The informal interviews elicited a very good response. Although they were extremely time-consuming, they obtained a clear picture of where provision is delivered, where collaboration would be beneficial and where duplication of provision is occurring. The information gathered was used to create maps of formal academic-led provision, formal student-led provision, and formal embedded provision.

Thirty responses were received to the surveys at York St John, with fifteen being from library and information personnel and the rest from academic personnel. No responses were received from other 'support' services. It was very soon evident that the responses to the online surveys were less complete and contained little or no reflection on provision, delivery and collaboration and more emphasis on providing bare facts. The results of the surveys were again used to create maps of formal delivery but it was not possible to differentiate between student-led, academic-led and embedded provision, or indeed whether provision was mandatory.

The importance of semantics and tailoring the questions to the recipients was very evident. For example, one respondent felt unable to answer any questions relating to the words 'support' or 'help' for students, as they felt that was not their role. It would seem that a sound knowledge of the culture and terminology of an institution is vital to eliciting useful responses. It is doubtful that any survey could produce responses as complete as those obtained by interviews, but what was obtained would provide a sound basis for further investigation.

Findings

The results from the audit could be used in a variety of ways, for example to identify:

- duplication of provision, in which case collaboration and shared delivery can be encouraged
- areas which have insufficient, or no, provision, which require action
- good practice, which can be shared across the institution
- individual or group training requirements, where skills are not available
- the role within an HEI best placed to take the curriculum forward
- resources required for adequate provision
- possible barriers to provision and methods for overcoming them.

An area of possible concern was the low level of support of students in Strand Seven (the ethical use of information) by those working in academic libraries, although a significantly higher proportion stated that they did support students in understand ethical issues such as plagiarism and copyright. This may indicate a lack of understanding of the term 'ethical dimension of information'; however, it may also suggest that this is not an area where students are getting adequate support.

The reluctance, and sometimes refusal, of some participants to engage with a survey that used terminology such as 'supporting students' and 'helping students' is also a concern, and might merit further investigation to identify whether it is an issue of semantics or whether some people in HEIs really believe it is not their role to help or support their students.

Before any audit is undertaken the management in each department must be fully informed, aware, and in agreement with the aims and outcomes of the process. This will ensure not only their support, but that of their teams, whose members will be prepared and willing to participate. Both the pilot audits were carried out in a very short timescale. This would not be recommended procedure, as a good deal of time is needed to plan, create, schedule and disseminate the surveys, or carry out the interviews, and then to assess the outcomes.

The involvement of partners with a wide knowledge of the HEI is extremely important, to identify suitable participants, market the audit to colleagues and ensure collaboration. The identification of possible issues with semantics in individual institutions should then be possible at an early stage to prevent misunderstandings and non-participation.

It is recommended that, whenever possible, interviews are undertaken in preference to questionnaires being distributed, as it was interesting – although perhaps not surprising – to note that the interviews elicited a fuller response. Interviewees also spent a considerable amount of time reflecting on their own roles and how they provide information literacy education, how that could be adapted, who they could work with and whether collaborative provision could be strengthened. The surveys, in contrast, were not always fully completed, perhaps due to misinterpretation of the questions, and answers were not expanded on in a reflective manner. However, interviews are obviously more demanding on time and require a suitable environment in which they can be conducted.

Project wiki

An unexpected outcome of the project was the Implementing ANCIL wiki.[2] Several of those who took part in the pilots expressed a need for an informal, accessible online space which could be used to find information about ANCIL and the documentation surrounding the curriculum. They also identified a need for this space to cover provision of information literacy education in universities generally, discuss issues, share best practice and resources, and find the project outcomes. The consensus was that it should be a space that all those involved in delivering information literacy could share and use, whatever their discipline.

The wiki was created on a free platform, and contains much of the body of this report and sections covering:

* Introduction
* Why information literacy needs a curriculum
* ANCIL
* Using ANCIL as a skills audit tool
  — Using ANCIL as a skills audit tool: skills audit questions
  — Using ANCIL as a skills audit tool: response to ancillary questions

— Using ANCIL as a skills audit tool: University of Worcester Case Study
— Using ANCIL as a skills audit tool: York St John University Case Study
- Implementing ANCIL: training
- Tools
- Resources
- Resources for University of Cambridge supervisors
- Resources for University of Cambridge colleges
- Information Literacy First Aid Model
- Ideas exchange.

The future of ANCIL

It is clear from the results of the pilots that ANCIL is a viable tool for creating an audit of the provision of information literacy skills within an HEI institution other than the University of Cambridge. While it was necessary to expand the basic strands and include questions covering their component parts, all those involved recognized at least part of their own delivery within the content. The fact that the questions prompted reflection and assessment on their own and their institutions' delivery of teaching and support, and the identification of opportunities for collaboration and improved provision, endorses the importance and validity of the new curriculum. As of now ANCIL is being used to audit provision at the London School of Economics and Political Science, which is reviewing provision for its undergraduate students and carrying out interviews and a survey.

One of the more surprising results of the research was caused by one survey respondent's answer to the question 'Who "owns" the information literacy support and teaching?' The reply was simply 'Ownership is a flawed concept.' My initial reaction was that this was a flippant response from somebody who was being asked to complete yet another survey. Then I thought more carefully about what that phrase means, and realized it defines what ANCIL is partly aimed at achieving.

Information literacy provision is not about spoon-feeding students with exactly what they need to pass a specific course: it is about teaching them how to use a spoon to feed themselves, and in time to differentiate between when they need a spoon and when a fork or a knife would be more appropriate. It is about supporting them in developing their own abilities, which they can apply not only to their academic work as undergraduates, but throughout their lives as productive, responsible and ethical members of the wider community. It is about ensuring that the provision they need is available at the right time, in the right format to build and support their information literacy. It is about librarians working with all the other professionals in an institution to share experience, skills and resources to deliver an integrated, holistic information literacy curriculum, which is as much a part of the student experience as their subject specific learning. It is about lighting a flame of enquiry that will shed light on a lifetime of information use.

Notes

1   http://arcadiaproject.lib.cam.ac.uk/projects/strategies-for-implementation.html.
2   http://implementingancil.pbworks.com.

Bibliography

Biddiscombe, R. (1999) Developing the Learning Support Role: some of the challenges ahead, *SCONUL Newsletter*, **16**, Spring, 30–4.

Coonan, E. and Secker, J. (2011) *A New Curriculum for Information Literacy: executive summary*, http://newcurriculum.wordpress.com/project-reports-and-outputs/.

Farkas, M. (2012) Participatory Technologies, Pedagogy 2.0 and Information Literacy, *Library Hi Tech*, **30** (1), 82–94.

McCluskey, C. (2011) Creating Information Literacy Partnerships in Higher Education [PowerPoint], www.slideshare.net/claremccluskey/lilac-presentation-2011.

Oxford, S. (2011) Making the Link and Seizing Opportunities: the PGCert and my development as a teacher (so far) [PowerPoint], http://lilacconference.com/WP/past-conferences/lilac-2011/.

Piloiu, R. (2011) Who Teaches Information Literacy?, Courtright Memorial Library, Otterbein University, http://otterbein.libguides.com/content.php?pid=127135&sid=1091824.

SCONUL Information Skills Task Force (1999) *Information Skills in Higher Education: a SCONUL position paper prepared by the SCONUL Advisory Committee on Information Literacy*, www.sconul.ac.uk/groups/information_literacy/papers/seven_pillars.html.

UNESCO (2005) Beacons of the Information Society: the Alexandria Proclamation on information literacy and lifelong learning, http://archive.ifla.org/III/wsis/BeaconInfSoc.html.

Conclusion

[O]ur society and all of its institutions are in continuing processes of transformation. . . . We must learn to understand, guide, influence and manage these transformations. We must make the capacity for undertaking them integral to ourselves and to our institutions. We must, in other words, become adept at learning.

Schon (1973, 28)

One of the greatest challenges for education has always been to help students to develop a questioning mind – an outlook which necessitates a critical approach to dealing with information and the capacity to evaluate and synthesize multiple perspectives on an issue. It also involves an understanding of how information is transformed into knowledge, and a recognition that learning is sometimes a challenging process, as it may involve assimilating new knowledge that challenges our world view.

In earlier times, information, knowledge and learning were privileged and scarce commodities accessible only to an elite, and controlled and mediated by teachers, librarians and other 'gatekeepers'. In the digital age, however, there is an abundance of information: knowledge and learning are more widely accessible than ever before, often in an unmediated form. The role of the librarian may be slowly evolving from the gatekeeper of knowledge, to a facilitator of learning, helping develop autonomy in students and impart a capacity for lifelong learning. Conversely, however, teachers and faculty observe that students, rather than becoming more independent in their approach to learning and more critical of the information they find, seem to be becoming less questioning and more dependent on teachers.

The central role that information and knowledge plays in learning means that in any discipline there needs to be an explicit approach to dealing with them. In the library world we call that capability 'information literacy'. Librarians are the natural partners to work with teachers to develop this learning framework in students, and to embed its development into the curriculum. This task is too big for one group in education to tackle alone and only by working together can we create a truly learner-focused environment. Yet perhaps the greatest challenge in the coming few years for those in the information and library profession is one of status and perceptions about their role. It is imperative that teachers and educators recognize the importance of an information literacy curriculum, embedded but explicit in the curriculum of all academic disciplines. It is also important that librarians make explicit the role they play in developing information literacies. We hope that this book has shown a way forward to developing reflective and critical abilities in students of the future in all disciplines.

We return to a question asked at the outset of this book: does teaching information literacy provide a new role for librarians in the digital age, and might it be the saviour of the library? Some might say that this book is a rallying cry to librarians in all sectors to shift information literacy into the core of their role in the future. And partly it is. However, information literacy cannot remain the preserve of the librarian if it is to be truly embedded in curricula across the different levels of education. Librarians might lead on information literacy in some institutions; however, they must work in partnership with teachers, with faculty and academics, and with other professionals in their institution, whether they be careers advisers, learning developers or instructional designers. They must also ensure that students recognize the value of information literacy, not just in their academic studies but also in their future lives and careers, in which learning will continue to play a key role. And, most importantly, information literacy must be recognized at the highest level in institutions as being a responsibility that all of us who work in education must jointly own.

The case studies presented in this book are deliberately different in their style, with each author providing an individual perspective on how one of the strands reflects their own practice. While each case reflected a specific institutional context, we hope that these examples of good practice will inspire practitioners and provide evidence of teaching that embodies aspects of the curriculum. ANCIL was designed to be flexible and adaptable, and so in each case study we have an individual perspective on how a strand might work in practice. So for example, Sarah Pavey's view of Strand One's content highlights work that she and her teaching colleagues are doing at the school level to bridge the transition to a different learning culture that students have to make on entering higher education. Meanwhile, the reflective exercises Helen Webster describes for Strand Ten address the corresponding transition out of the formal education environment and into the social dimension of information, or lifelong learning.

Many case studies show how the ten strands complement or dovetail with one another. For Strands Five and Six, Isla Kuhn and Elizabeth Tilley show in different yet complementary ways how the 'bread and butter' information literacy teaching that many librarians are already doing can be enriched. Both contextualize a particular skill within the broader information handling framework, showing how resource evaluation and reference management can be used to teach students about the finer points of finding, evaluating and managing information.

Meanwhile, Strand Eight from Andy Priestner showcases how new digital media such as blogs and Twitter can be used by researchers for communicating and presenting information. This is a strand where the needs of the disciplines will largely dictate some of the tools and techniques that students explore. In contrast, Emma Coonan's session for Strand Nine illustrates how exploring the practices of academic reading and writing across different disciplines can help students to make reflective connections between their own experiences of writing, thinking and problem framing and the often unexplained conventions and expectations of the academic environment.

Interprofessional collaboration is crucial to ANCIL, and Katy Wrathall's Afterword shows some of the tensions, opportunities and revelations that its implementation might raise. However, several of our authors demonstrate that this collaboration is already taking place in various institutions and at various levels. Lyn Parker describes a whole-institution approach to the ethical issues around information (Strand Seven), in which the library takes a leading strategic role. For Strand Three Moira Bent similarly outlines how the library is working at institutional level to support academics' developing understanding of the interrelation between academic and information literacies.

Partnership and an enhanced understanding of the value that librarians can offer in a digital age are key to both Geoff Walton and Jamie Cleland's teaching and to that of Clare McCluskey (Strands Two and Four). These authors have worked closely with academic partners on designing as well as delivering module content, and each has facilitated deeper communication across the professions, creating a community of practice with shared aims and values.

Each of our case studies therefore illustrates a strand of ANCIL, but it is the value of bringing together these components in a curriculum that has the power to really be transformative. We hope that through the case studies this book explores ANCIL in practice and illustrates how the new curriculum is different from previous models and standards of information literacy. ANCIL is not a ten-module course, nor a competency framework against which to measure learners' development. There is no 'old curriculum' that the new curriculum is based on. It is in essence different because of being a curriculum, and also because it was designed using Biggs' notion of 'constructive alignment' (1996), which argues that the knowledge, skills and behaviour of students must be aligned with both the learning outcomes and the assessment methods employed. ANCIL offers a way to re-conceptualize information literacy and to situate it as a central part of any academic discipline. We believe that our case studies reflect and celebrate the different implementations of our information literacy curriculum, and that, when read together, the combined output is greater than the sums of the parts.

Finally, it is worth re-emphasizing that much of what our practitioners have described is not work developed as a response to ANCIL but existing good practice that predates the research. The curriculum was developed in consultation with many of the practitioners who contributed to this book, so the case studies provide evidence that there is a new way of thinking about information literacy. While each case study on its own is interesting, it is only by reading them all that the full breadth of the curriculum can be appreciated. ANCIL was developed iteratively, with good practice from the profession informing and inspiring the research that developed the curriculum. Through workshops, dissemination on the website and not least this book, we hope to see ANCIL having an impact on practitioners and on the work that is going on to develop information literacy more broadly in the education sector.

In addition to the case studies, we have developed a range of tools to help practitioners further. These final sections of the book comprise:

- Appendix 1, which contains the complete curriculum, with learning outcomes, sample activities and assessments
- Appendix 2, which provides a lesson plan to help you structure a class or session that you run and plan it according to ANCIL
- Appendices 3 and 4, which offer a means of auditing information literacy provision across your institution.

We welcome your thoughts and feedback, and please do consider sharing your approach to reshaping and rethinking information literacy via our website, http://newcurriculum.wordpress.com, or via our wiki, http://implementingancil.pbworks.com.

Bibliography

Biggs, J. (1996) Enhancing Teaching Through Constructive Alignment, *Higher Education*, **32** (3), 347–64.

Schon, D. (1973) *Beyond the Stable State: public and private learning in a changing society*, Penguin Books.

Appendix 1

A New Curriculum for Information Literacy (ANCIL): the curriculum

Strand 1 Transition from school to higher education			
Strand content	Learning outcomes	Example activities	Example assessment
What are the expectations at higher education level in your discipline?	Distinguish between the expectations at school and HE level in your discipline Recognise that learning at HE is different and requires different strategies Identify and assess the range of information formats available	Tutor outlines contrasting expectations at secondary and HE levels Students review examples of HE level work at school and discuss differences with their prior work Classroom-based activity to explore and contrast how information on a relevant topic is presented in monographs, journals, reports and other formats	Short reflective piece of writing on transition issues – students identifies areas they need to address (ideally assessed by personal tutor or academic)
What are the conventions around reading, writing and presenting at higher education level in your discipline?	Develop an awareness of academic conventions at HE level Assess your reading, writing and presenting skills and compare them to experts within your discipline	What makes an academic journal article different from an article in a publication like *History Today* or *New Scientist*? Identify the differences in presentation, attribution, tone of voice, etc.; discuss why those genre conventions are used – what purpose do they achieve? Discuss what a basic descriptive answer might be and what would need to be added to take a more analytical approach	Rewrite a paragraph from a popular publication as though for an academic audience (for peer assessment)
Reflect on your current and previous information behaviour – what's different?	Assess your current information-seeking behaviour and compare it to experts within your discipline Critique the tools and strategies you currently use to find scholarly information Evaluate the information environment including libraries and digital libraries as 'trusted' collections	Using reading lists as a starting point, identify the key types of information that are important in your discipline – discuss those you are familiar with and those you have not used before Identify your top 3 (or 5) current information sources and evaluate their fitness for purpose in line with academic expectations – create a mind-map of your information landscape as it currently appears and share with peers	Postcard from the edge: identify 3 new strategies, tools or sources that you found useful in class and write yourself a postcard Class leader to send cards after e.g. 1 week

Strand 2 Becoming an independent learner			
Strand content	Learning outcomes	Example activities	Example assessment
Learning to learn	Reflect on how to create strategies for assimilating new knowledge Identify your learning style and preferences, including specific learning needs	Arrange verbs from Bloom's Taxonomy on a scale into higher- and lower-order skills	*Use activity as formative assessment*
Affective dimension of information literacy	Critique the concept that learning changes the learner Acknowledge the emotional impact of learning on your worldview	Students reflect on a positive and a negative learning experience and discuss why one worked and one didn't How did you cope with the negative experience? How did you take forward the positive?	Demonstrate an awareness of sources of support at all levels in your institution A case study exercise to diagnose the issues: what advice would you give, and where would you refer the person?

Strand 3 Developing academic literacies			
Strand content	Learning outcomes	Example activities	Example assessment
Academic writing, rhetoric and persuasive writing	Identify appropriate terminology, use of language and academic idiom in your discipline Identify overt and implicit techniques for influencing the reader/viewer in different arenas – in academic writing, in advertising, in the media Develop an awareness of the epistemological structure and values in your discipline	Assess and compare the quality of 3 short pieces of writing (one deliberately flawed) Compare writing style, structure, and use of evidence across a range of papers on the same topic – students vote for best paper and discuss why it met their criteria Analyse the structure of a key work in your discipline and break it down into component parts: does it convince you? Why?	Marks in first-year assignments explicitly awarded for academic writing abilities The elevator challenge – pitch an argument to someone you want to convince in two minutes Students vote for best elevator pitch and discuss why it met their criteria
Academic reading, critical analysis and textual interrogation	Learn the techniques of skimming and scanning Identify the strengths and weaknesses of source material Evaluate the place of source material within the wider debate	Summarise the key arguments in a monograph after being given 20 minutes to read it; discuss the different strategies adopted, e.g. using the index, reading the introduction and conclusion Locate key information in a text which is not really about that topic, but does contain useful snippets Discuss what it means to critique a text – i.e. not necessarily finding fault with everything; list the key evaluative criteria you would apply to texts in your field in order to establish their relative value and contribution Evaluate critical appraisal tools (e.g. CASP, peer review reporting, journal referee guidelines) and discuss their value and potential application in your discipline	Timed exercise – skimming for key information: peer assess in pairs Write a critical review of a subject-appropriate text (part of formal course assessment)

Strand 4 Mapping and evaluating the information landscape			
Strand content	Learning outcomes	Example activities	Example assessment
Identify trusted source formats	Select appropriate resources for your assignment, discriminating between good quality academic sources and other sources Develop evaluative criteria for recognising and selecting trustworthy sources of academic quality in your discipline	Students explore a number of sources – for instance real and spoof websites (e.g. www.dhmo.org/) – and consider how they identify trustworthy sources Compare a subject entry in Wikipedia with an entry in a non-current encyclopedia and discuss their relative value Examine monographs, journals, reports and other formats	Devise a list of criteria for assessing trustworthiness and credibility of source formats Students locate a book, a journal article and a website not on their reading list and consider in pairs the relative value of what they have found to their assignment
Who are the experts in the field? How do we know?	Identify the key experts in your field Analyse what makes an expert in your discipline	Choose a noteworthy author in the discipline and evaluate his/her impact through citations – does this author qualify as an expert? Justify	Tutor feeds back on student evaluation of expertise
Evaluating source material and its appropriateness for your specific purpose	Use information sources appropriately to develop or support your argument Develop evaluative criteria for assessing ways of using source material in your work	Distinguish and discuss how you might use source material (to check facts, to grasp background information, to support your argument, to undermine someone else's argument ...) Look at a sample text and categorise the reasons why they have used source material	Marks in first-year assignments explicitly awarded for appropriate use of evidence and sources

Strand 5 Resource discovery in your discipline			
Strand content	Learning outcomes	Example activities	Example assessment
Using key finding aids in your discipline	Identify key finding aids in your discipline – e.g. catalogues, full-text databases, abstract and indexing services Develop strategies for using them	Discuss the differences between academic finding aids and freely available search engines (e.g. will Google tell you what books are in the library?) List the different types of information you need to find out, and match them up with the various aids – which fits your need best?	
Going beyond the key finding aids	Identify subject-specific collections of information such as gateways and portals Develop strategies for using them	Evaluate a subject-specific resource new to you and identify how it fits into your information landscape (discuss or mind-map)	
Finding and using specialist forms of information	Identify the types of specialist information common in your discipline – e.g. datasets, statistics, archival evidence Develop strategies for using them, including awareness of sources of expert help	Give students some raw data and ask them to identify what subject disciplines might use it, and how Would it be useful for your own subject? Locate sources of data that fall outside your field and discuss how they might be helpful (e.g. a historical dataset for studying literature)	*Appropriate assessments must be developed and carried out by or in collaboration with faculty members*
Finding and using people as information sources	Identify the strengths of people in your personal network – peers, academic staff, and others – as sources of information Evaluate the strengths of online user-generated content as sources of information	Discuss the relative value of using social media (e.g. blogs/Facebook/Twitter) as a source of information Choose a prominent, networked scholar and explore his/her academic research, popular profile, and use of social media	

Strand 6 Managing information			
Strand content	Learning outcomes	Example activities	Example assessment
Note-taking	Distinguish between note-taking (dictation) and note-making (considered retention of vital points) Develop a strategy for note-making – in lectures/supervisions, for your reading, in everyday situations	Listen to short (e.g. 2 minute) podcast and make: 1) as full a transcript as possible; 2) notes of salient points Reflect on ease and relative value of both approaches Identify which parts of your notes reflect the original content and which are related to your own thinking – Evaluate the strategies you use to distinguish different types of notes	Peer discussion and assessment
Time management and planning	Produce a strategy to manage your workload Evaluate your own learning and working styles	Create a plan including deadlines and a realistic time frame for your next piece of assessed work/across the whole term Assess your learning and working styles and identify areas of weakness	Include plan with submitted assignment – discuss with tutor and reflect on value
Storing information effectively	Develop and implement a plan for organising your files (including naming and organising folders) Decide on an appropriate information management technique suitable for your discipline / the resources you use	Devise a system for storing a number of files prepared by session leader – including some variant versions, e.g. tutor comments on an essay draft Explore cloud storage tools and discuss the merits of remote vs local storage, online vs paper storage – list potential hazards!	Peer assessment – students discuss, compare and rank their current strategies
Bibliographic and reference management	Identify and use an appropriate citation style in your assignments Construct appropriate bibliographies for your assignments Evaluate reference management tools and strategies in the light of your own workflow	Hands-on comparison and exploration of free and paid for reference management software; write a review of different software for other students Discuss the merits of different reference management strategies (e.g. software vs paper storage) – list potential hazards	Timed assessment in class – generate an appropriately formatted bibliography from a reference list supplied by class leader, using the tool of your choice
Push services / alerting / keeping up to date	Develop appropriate strategies for current awareness in your field	Identify and evaluate various of alert services – RSS, e-mail alerts, aggregators, etc.	Short reflective piece describing whether and how you will use alert services – and how you'll store and organise the information they generate

Strand 7 Ethical dimension of information			
Strand content	Learning outcomes	Example activities	Example assessment
Attribution and avoiding plagiarism	Identify the steps you can take to avoid plagiarism, deliberate or inadvertent Use correct academic practices in quoting, citing and paraphrasing	Discuss the need to attribute quotations, paraphrases and ideas appropriately Identify why plagiarism might happen and categorise the types of poor academic practice that lead to plagiarism Plagiarise deliberately and pass to another student to put it right	Marks in first-year assignments explicitly awarded for bibliographies and appropriate attribution
Sharing information appropriately	Summarise the key ways you can use and share information without infringing another's rights Distinguish between collaboration and collusion Compare dissemination practices in your discipline across a range of publication platforms (preprint repositories, blogs, bibliographic sharing services, etc.)	Students are asked to find suitable images for use in a class presentation – introduce concept of Creative Commons Examine a number of scenarios to determine which constitute collusion	Marks are awarded for the appropriate use of image and video sources in student presentations
Awareness of copyright and IPR issues	Develop an awareness of how copyright and IPR issues impact on your work Develop strategies as appropriate for working within the legal framework	Students discuss the role of copyright laws in protecting musicians, artists and file makers Reflect on how copyright laws have impacted on them either socially or academically Examine a number of scenarios to determine which constitute copyright infringement	Students work together to develop a policy or guidelines for their institution that reflects real practice and complies with legal issues Assessment by Copyright Officer/IPR specialist

Strand 8 Presenting and communicating knowledge			
Strand content	Learning outcomes	Example activities	Example assessment
Finding your voice	Use language appropriately in your academic writing Analyse competing arguments and the use of evidence to justify a position	Practise writing in first and third person Discuss appropriate use of language for your audience Comment critically on the views of others, so your voice is distinguished – working in pairs, swap and critique	*Use activity as formative assessment*
Managing your online identity and digital footprint	Develop an awareness of how you appear to others online Decide on appropriate level of information to communicate to different audiences (i.e .manage your digital footprint) Evaluate the suitability of different online locations/tools for your online presence	Working in pairs, Google each other and assemble a profile of the other person, including any negative information Consider your own profile as a 'produser' – how much of a trail do you leave by consuming information online?	*Use activity as formative assessment*
Communicating your findings appropriately	Choose an appropriate writing style, level and format for your intended audience Summarise the key methods of publishing research findings in your discipline (including self-publication, e.g. blogging) Assess the relationship between writing style, audience and publication platform	Students look at how information on a topical issue in their discipline e.g. climate change is presented in newspapers, on websites and in academic journals and discuss the key differences	Write different short pieces communicating the same information to different audiences for different reasons

Strand 9 Synthesising information and creating new knowledge			
Strand content	Learning outcomes	Example activities	Example assessment
Formulating research questions and framing problems	Use chosen information sources to articulate and analyse new problems in your field	Discuss paradigm shifts in your field (tutor input) – e.g. impact of quantum theory on Newtonian physics Discuss new ways of framing questions or approaching issues in the field (potentially in the context of your dissertation topic)	Assessment involves a set of marks awarded for innovation and creativity when framing problems Students work on creating their own research questions (tutor feedback needed)
Assimilating information within the disciplinary framework	Assess the value of new information objectively in the context of your work Develop new insights and knowledge in your discipline	In pairs students are given a broad topic (e.g. climate change) and asked to prepare a for/against argument Students debate issue and a vote is taken Marks awarded for use of evidence to support arguments	Second and third year assessments are explicit about how marks are awarded for assimilation of ideas

Strand 10 Social dimension of information			
Strand content	Learning outcomes	Example activities	Example assessment
Becoming a lifelong learner	Develop an awareness that learning is a continuous ongoing process outside of formal educational establishments Develop strategies for assimilating new information to the conceptual framework	Discuss the statement 'When the facts change, I change my opinion' in the light of choosing whether and how to vote in a general election Reflect on how you have changed as a learner since school	*Use activity as formative assessment*
Information handling, problem solving and decision making in the workplace	Transfer the skills of finding, critically evaluating, and deploying information to the workplace	Without using any subscription resources, students search for information to answer a specific query They carry out the same search to compare the information they can find using paid for resources Find information to help you handle a change management scenario in the workplace	*Use activity as formative assessment*
Information handling, problem solving and decision making in your daily life	Transfer the skills of finding, critically evaluating, and deploying information to daily life	Reflect on the best way to choose an energy supplier using discussion and internet sources to help you Discuss the trust value of cost comparison websites	*Use activity as formative assessment*
Ethics and politics of information	Develop strategies for assimilating and analysing new information, including that which challenges your world view	Presentation of sensitive or nuanced information in the press – compare how the same story is reported in a tabloid, a broadsheet and in various news sources	*Use activity as formative assessment*

Appendix 2

ANCIL Lesson Plan

Course title:
Purpose – *what study or research need will be met?*
Target audience
Learning outcome(s) – *what will participants know or be able to do by the end of the session? (You should start each point with a verb!)* •   •   • •   •   •
ANCIL learning bands Practical skill • Subject context • Advanced information-handling • Learning to learn •
Practicalities
Format and duration of session
Venue layout
Equipment needed
Content
Materials
Active and reflective components – *what will the participants do to reinforce or explore what they learn?*
Assessment and feedback mechanism – *formative and/or summative*
The institutional picture
Which ANCIL strands are represented in the session content?
Where does this session dovetail or overlap with other provision in the institution?

Appendix 3

ANCIL Institutional Audit: worksheet

Use this form to map out which departments, services or individuals in your institution provide support for students within each strand and in what format. (If you find it helpful, concentrate on provision targeted at one group of students, e.g. undergraduates in a specific department or faculty.)

	Formal training	Ad-hoc or informal consultations	Online support	Other, e.g. leaflets
Strand One: Transition to HE Clarifying the differences in expectation and practice between school and university				
Strand Two: Becoming an independent learner Opportunities for students to reflect on, enhance and manage their own learning, including its emotional impact				
Strand Three: Developing academic literacies All aspects of academic reading and writing, including critical analysis, framing arguments, style and structure				
Strand Four: Mapping the landscape Evaluating scholarly material, identifying trusted source formats, recognising expertise in a given discipline				
Strand Five: Resource discovery Recognising the key finding aids, and going beyond them to using specialist information sources (e.g. datasets, archives)				
Strand Six: Managing information Developing key skills: note-making, time management, information storage, reference management, alerting services				
Strand Seven: Ethical dimension of information Understanding attribution and how to avoid plagiarism; copyright, IPR, appropriate levels of sharing				
Strand Eight: Presenting and communication Choosing an appropriate voice, style, level and format to communicate various types of scholarly output; managing online identity				
Strand Nine: Creating new knowledge Assimilating and synthesising information within a disciplinary context, framing problems, formulating research questions				
Strand Ten: Social dimension of information Translating learned experience into dealing with information needs in new contexts, e.g. workplace, daily life				

Appendix 4

ANCIL Institutional Audit: interview questions

These questions were used in the pilot audit undertaken at York St John University and University of Worcester. They may be used in interviews (this is the recommended data collection method), and may also be adapted for use as a questionnaire.

1. What is your job title?

2. How would you summarise your role?

3. Do you support students?

4. At which point(s) do you support them?
   4.1   Throughout their time in higher education
   4.2   At transition
   4.3   At first year
   4.4   At second year
   4.5   At third year
   4.6   At postgraduate level
   4.7   At leaving

5. These are the strands of the new curriculum. Does your role involve delivering provision or supporting students formally within any of them at the moment?
   5.1   Transition to higher education
   5.2   Becoming an independent learner
   5.3   Developing academic literacies
   5.4   Mapping and evaluating the information landscape
   5.5   Resource discovery in a set discipline

5.6   Managing information
5.7   Ethical dimension of information
5.8   Presenting and communicating information
5.9   Synthesising information and creating new knowledge
5.10   Social dimension of information

6.   **Where 'formally' means timetabled sessions that students have to attend, and 'informally' means non-compulsory sessions, online materials or other support, do you formally or informally:**
6.1   Help students produce work at HE level
6.2   Help students differentiate between a popular and an academic resource
6.3   Help students find their academic voice
6.4   Help students work out how to find resources and understand the process
6.5   Help students think about how they research and why
6.6   Help students identify how they learn and what strategies they can use
6.7   Help students deal with negative learning experiences
6.8   Help students identify support available
6.9   Help students learn to influence through use of language
6.10   Help students understand how they are influenced
6.11   Help students develop reading techniques like skimming
6.12   Help students learn they can find relevant information in a resource that isn't apparently about their topic
6.13   Help students develop evaluation skills
6.14   Help students learn who their subject experts are and why
6.15   Help students muster their argument with supporting evidence
6.16   Help students know what the best tools are for them to use
6.17   Help students explore new 'finding aids'
6.18   Help students know key people to go to, including their peers
6.19   Help students develop note-taking skills
6.20   Help students manage their time
6.21   Help students plan
6.22   Help students develop an information-handling strategy (e.g. using folders, etc.)
6.23   Help students with citations and referencing

6.24   Help students use current awareness strategies

6.25   Help students understand and avoid plagiarism

6.26   Help students understand the ethics of information use

6.27   Help students understand copyright issues

6.28   Help students understand and manage their online presence and digital footprint

6.29   Help students use the right tone for different occasions

6.30   Help students formulate research questions

6.31   Help students evaluate new information

6.32   Help students realise learning is ongoing

6.33   Help students transfer their skills to the workplace

6.34   Help students be open-minded about new information

7. **Who do you work with informally to deliver these outcomes?**

8. **Who would you like to work with in your organisation?**

9. **Who owns the information literacy support and teaching?**

10. **Who do you think should own this provision?**

11. **How should the New Curriculum be delivered?**

12. **Could it be delivered collaboratively?**

13. **Who would be on your side?**

14. **Who might get in your way or need further convincing?**

15. **What other challenges might you face?**

16. **What would you need to support you when implementing the curriculum (e.g. resources)?**

17. **Who are the top three people to get on side in your organisation?**

Index

Copyright and E-learning
A guide for practitioners
Jane Secker

'fluent, well-paced, accessible and user-friendly... it would be a useful addition to the arsenal of resources for anyone working in the copyright and elearning arena.'
Journal of Information Literacy

Copyright is frequently seen as a barrier to making materials available in e-learning environments. Through its practically based overview of current and emerging copyright issues facing those working in the field of e-learning, this book will help to break this barrier down and equip professionals with the tools, skills and understanding they need to work confidently and effectively in the virtual learning environment with the knowledge that they are doing so legally.

Fully supported with a broad range of practitioner case studies and further sources of information, this essential guide looks at best practice developed by leading universities in the UK and overseas which support students in a blended learning environment. Key topics include:

- the background to copyright and e-learning
- digitizing published content for delivery in the VLE
- using multimedia in e-learning
- copyright issues and 'born' digital resources
- copyright in the emerging digital environment of Web 2.0
- copyright training for staff.

This book is essential reading for anyone working in education including learning support staff and teachers using e-learning, learning technologists, librarians, educational developers, instructional designers, IT staff and trainers. It is also relevant for anyone working in the education sector from school level to higher education, and those developing learning resources in commercial organizations and the public sector including libraries, museums and archives, and government departments.

2010; 224pp; paperback; 978-1-85604-665-7; £49.95

A Guide to Teaching Information Literacy
101 practical tips
Helen Blanchett, Chris Powis and Jo Webb

'... this is an essential book for those new to teaching information literacy, and a useful addition to the collection of experienced practitioners. It is certainly one to which I will return in the future.'

Journal of Information Literacy

This book is a much-needed sourcebook to support library staff in the delivery of information literacy teaching, by providing practical guidance on tried and tested ideas and techniques for sessions. Full of hints and tips grounded in learning theory, it is a practical reference tool designed to be dipped into as needed when planning teaching and training. Where applicable the activities are mapped to models of information literacy, with guidance on adapting ideas for different levels and contexts.

Advice is given on activities in the following areas:

- designing sessions
- preparing sessions
- delivering sessions
- different types of sessions
- teaching by topic
- creating teaching / support materials
- assessing learning
- evaluating teaching sessions
- e-learning.

This easy-to-use book is an invaluable source of inspiration for any librarian involved in teaching information literacy, whether they are new to teaching or experienced but in search of fresh ideas.

2011; 256pp; paperback; 978-1-85604-659-6; £49.95

Information Literacy Meets Library 2.0
Peter Godwin and Jo Parker, editors

Web 2.0 technologies have been seen by many information professionals as critical to the development of library services, leading to the use of the term Library 2.0 to denote the kind of service envisaged. There has been much debate about what Library 2.0 might encompass, but, in the context of information literacy, it can be described as the application of interactive, collaborative, and multimedia technologies to web-based library services and collections.

These developments challenge librarians involved in information literacy with more complex and diverse web content, a range of exciting new tools with which to teach, and a steep learning curve to adjust to the constant change of the Web 2.0 world.

This edited collection from an international team of experts provides a practically-based overview of emerging Library 2.0 tools and technologies for information literacy practitioners; addresses the impact of the adoption of these technologies on information literacy teaching; provides case study exemplars for practitioners to help inform their practice; and examines the implications of Library 2.0 for the training of information literacy professionals. Key topics include:

- School Library 2.0: new skills and knowledge for the future
- information literacy, Web 2.0 and public libraries
- the blog as an assessment tool
- using Wikipedia to eavesdrop on the scholarly conversation
- information literacy and RSS feeds
- library instruction on the go: podcasting
- sparking Flickrs of insight into controlled vocabularies and subject searching
- joining the YouTube conversation to teach information literacy
- going beyond Google
- teaching information literacy through digital games.

This book will be essential reading for all library and information practitioners and policy makers with responsibility for developing and delivering information literacy programmes to their users.

2008; 200pp; hardback; 978-1-85604-637-4: £49.95

Information Literacy Beyond Library 2.0
Peter Godwin and Jo Parker, editors

'This book is of most benefit to anyone teaching information literacy, and especially so to those involved in developing digital literacy skills in their user groups. It is also a great source of contacts and resources, providing names for information literacy proponents across the world.'

MANAGING INFORMATION

This new book picks up where the best-selling *Information Literacy Meets Library 2.0* left off. In the last three years the information environment has changed dramatically, becoming increasingly dominated by the social and the mobile. This new book asks where we are now, what is the same and what has changed, and, most crucially, how do we as information professionals respond to the new information literacy and become a central part of the revolution itself?

The book is divided into three distinct sections. Part 1 explores the most recent trends in technology, consumption and literacy, while Part 2 is a resource bank of international case studies that demonstrate the key trends and their effect on information literacy and offer innovative ideas to put into practice. Part 3 assesses the impact of these changes on librarians and what skills and knowledge they must acquire to evolve alongside their users.

Some of the key topics covered are:

- the evolution of 'online' into the social web as mainstream
- the use of social media tools in information literacy
- the impact of mobile devices on information literacy delivery
- shifting literacies, such as metaliteracy, transliteracy and media literacy, and their effect on information literacy.

This is essential reading offering practical strategies for all library and information practitioners and policy makers with responsibility for developing and delivering information literacy programmes to their users. It will also be of great interest to students of library and information studies particularly for modules relating to literacy, information behaviour and digital technologies.

March 2012; 256pp; paperback; 978-1-85604-762-3; £49.95